PRAYER LIFE

PRAYER LIFE

HOW YOUR PERSONALITY AFFECTS THE WAY YOU PRAY

PABLO MARTÍNEZ

First published in 2001 by Spring Harvest Publishing Division
and Paternoster Lifestyle

07 06 05 04 03 02 01   7 6 5 4 3 2 1

Paternoster Lifestyle is an imprint of Paternoster Publishing,
P.O. Box 300, Carlisle, Cumbria, CA3 0QS, UK
and Paternoster Publishing USA
Box 1047, Waynesboro, GA 30830-2047
www.paternoster-publishing.com

British Library Cataloguing in Publication Data

A catalogue record for this book is available from the British
Library

ISBN 1-85078-436-1

Cover design by Campsie
Printed in Great Britain by
Cox and Wyman, Cardiff Road, Reading

Contents

Contents

Author Profile

Pablo Martínez
Trained as a medical doctor and psychiatrist, Pablo Martínez works at a Christian hospital in Barcelona. Besides this professional activity he has developed a wide ministry as a lecturer and counsellor. He has been a guest speaker in more than twenty countries in Europe. Former President of the Spanish GBU (the equivalent of UCCF) for eight years, he is still very much involved with student ministry, especially in the areas of Bible exposition and apologetics. A member of the Executive Committee of the International Christian Medical and Dental Association (ICMDA), he is currently President of the Spanish Evangelical Alliance, and has been a speaker at Spring Harvest four times (1994, 1996, 1998 and 2001). He was one of the members of the founding council of the London Institute for Contemporary Christianity (1982) and Professor of Pastoral Theology at the Spanish Theological Seminary (1988-1995).

Foreword

I have enjoyed the friendship of Pablo Martínez for more than twenty years and am grateful for the opportunity to commend his book *Prayer Life* to a wide readership.

It is not difficult to pinpoint its special value. Here is a psychiatrist who is committed to Christ, knows his Bible, rejoices in Christ's cross, has a lively sympathy for struggling Christians and has much wisdom born of rich pastoral experience. These ingredients together make a strong mixture!

Dr Martínez accepts the Jungian distinction between extroverts and introverts, and his classification of four main psychological types. He is surely right to insist that our temperament is a genetic endowment, and that the new birth does not change it, although grace helps us to live with it and the Holy Spirit changes us into the like-ness of Christ. He urges us to discover who we are, and to accept and respect each other in the rich diversity of the human family. As we study his thorough portraiture of different psychological types, we soon recognize our-selves and our friends.

Next he comes to the practice of prayer and how our prayers are affected by our temperament and pesonality. There are different styles of prayer which suit different kinds of people; he is an enemy of all stereotypes. He also faces honestly some of the problems which Christians experience, and makes practical suggestions for solving them. He urges us to persevere, because of the therapeutic value of prayer.

But our author is also familiar with the contours of contemporary thought and knows about the current influences which are hostile to prayer. In his last two chapters he tackles these. He develops a robust defence both of the authenticity of Christian prayer, against the slander that it is mere auto-suggestion, and of the uniqueness of Christian prayer, against the claim that it is no different from Eastern meditation.

Pablo Martínez has written a profound, practical and personal book in which the skill of the psychiatrist and the gentleness of the pastor are combined. His overall aim is to encourage 'prayer without guilt'; he wants us to discover that prayer is 'more a pleasure than a burden'. I warmly commend this English edition. I cannot imagine any reader failing to be helped by it, as I have been myself.

John Stott
London, September 2001

Introduction

As I decided to write about how our personalities and character affect our prayer lives, three purposes were in my mind: first, to help the ordinary Christian who is struggling unnecessarily with their own prayer life and spirituality. Many Christians believe their struggles are sinful, not understanding that very often they are the result of their own emotional makeup. I would like my readers to think of prayer without guilt, because too often we associate the two together. Prayer should not be just one more burden in life, but a pleasure to enjoy.

My second purpose was to help Christians develop their prayer lives to their full potential, while understanding how these are affected by their temperaments and personalities. How do they affect our praying – and what can we do about it? How can I use the benefits and counteract the drawbacks of my character in prayer? I would like to promote mutual acceptance in our relationships, between individual Christians and between churches, as a result of grasping the basic principle that variety is a treasure than enriches, not an obstacle that bothers.

Third, I wanted to make clear the great therapeutic value of prayer. Prayer is a powerful tool to bring emotional healing into our lives. It is in prayer that we encounter, face to face, the supreme Physician, our Lord Jesus Christ, who wants to give us 'life abundantly' (Jn. 10:10).

The second part (chapters 4 and 5) is on the apologetics of prayer. Its purpose is to equip the reader with reasons for defending the relevance and uniqueness of Christian prayer in a postmodern society. This book is addressed to the evangelical community in general, rather than to the professional group of Christian psychologists and psychiatrists. For this reason, I have tried to avoid technical detail and to be very practical. The book has been forged mainly through direct contact with ordinary Christians, who answered questionnaires or accepted interviews, thus making an invaluable personal contribution.

Some words of gratitude are necessary here because this book is the result of many efforts. Ali Hull has been not only a very efficient editor, but a partner whose comments and suggestions have greatly enriched the book. Bob Horn was the person who first introduced me to Word Alive/Spring Harvest, and consequently opened the doors to the series of lectures which were the basis for the book. My wife, Marta, has given me essential help in practicalities of using a computer! Finally, I want to thank my parents from whom I learned that prayer, the spinal cord of our Christian life, is a pleasure to enjoy, a source of peace and blessing, much more than a burden. If I manage to help my readers to learn this same principle, the book will have accomplished its purpose.

Part 1

The Psychology of Prayer

Chapter 1

DIFFERENT PRAYERS FOR DIFFERENT PEOPLE

Prayer in relation to temperament

'Why do I find it difficult to pray?' 'Why do some Christians seem to have a natural ease when it comes to praying?' 'Why do I feel so hypocritical when I pray?' 'Why do I find it hard to feel the presence of God when I pray?' 'Is my problem a lack of faith?'

These frequently heard questions reflect an important reality: our prayers are not only affected by spiritual conditions but other things as well. There are three factors that have the most powerful effect on our prayer lives. Two of them have a permanent, continuous influence: our *temperament* and our *personality*. They are closely linked to our character, to what we are like as people. The third factor, the *circumstances* of the moment, depend on temporary phenomena: their effects only last for a certain length of time.

In the chapters that follow, I want to analyse the way in which these factors affect our prayer life on two levels: in the course of prayer, which we might call the flow or the dynamics of prayer, and in the content of prayer.

In other words, our temperament, our personality and our circumstances at a given moment affect *how we pray* and *what we pray*.

This does not mean that our prayer life is completely at the mercy of emotional and circumstantial factors. This view, that of psychological determinism, is a serious mistake that has been made by several different schools of psychology. Both the orthodox psychoanalysis of Freud and Skinner's behaviourism maintain that the mind regulates our behaviour and our whole lives so strongly that it leaves very little scope for other influences. We do believe, as Christians, that prayer is performed under the influence of the Holy Spirit and he assumes a central role throughout the entire course of prayer.

In analysing the psychological factors of prayer, I do not want to minimise the role of the One who 'intercedes for us with groans that words cannot express' (Rom. 8:26b), and so reduce it to that of an extra. Nothing could be farther from my intention. But it would also be a mistake to ignore the extraordinary influence that our psychological makeup has on our spiritual life in general and on our prayer life in particular.

Why do our temperament, our personality and our circumstances affect us so much? The answer is that man is a unity, that has basically three parts. The somatic part – our bodies, the mental part – our minds, the psyche – and our spirit, the pneuma. These three interact in such a way that when the body suffers, the mind is affected and so is the spirit. When Spurgeon, the famous preacher, was suffering from a severe attack of gout, he had severely disturbed moods. We might not imagine the prince of preachers being depressed, but such was the reality: a physical problem was affecting his mood – his psychological structure – and it may also have affected his preaching sometimes. We all know examples of this interaction between our different parts. In the same way, if our minds are affected by childhood traumas and injuries, if we come from broken families, if we feel anxious or inferior or insecure – all these things will affect our spiritual life.

We have to see man as a psycho-somatic-pneumatic unity, with no part being superior to the others. We cannot say that the mind is better than the spirit, or the body than the mind. This was one of the greatest mistakes of Platonism – Plato said that the body was the jail of the spirit. Therefore, according to biblical teaching, people are a unity of mind, body and spirit and these three are inextricably linked together. We cannot isolate any of these parts, just as we cannot isolate this psycho-somatic-spiritual whole from the influence of our surroundings. No one is so spiritual as to be able to claim that 'the psychological' does not affect them. That would be just as presumptuous and naïve as to claim 'I am pure spirit'. Some believers are so 'spiritual' that they even attribute the emotional part of the person to the fall. In fact, when God created humankind he didn't make people as mere spirits, without bodies or emotions. Our psychological dimension already existed before the presence of sin in the world. As Christians we believe that the opposite of what is spiritual is not what is human – the body or the mind – but what is carnal, being flesh. What puts out the Spirit's fire is not our human nature in itself, but our fleshly desires which are a result of sin.

The Lord Jesus Christ was the man par excellence, but he never claimed to be so spiritual that the outward circumstances did not affect him, nor to possess a kind of spirituality that was not integrated with the rest of him. Consider one of his most impressive prayers: Gethsemane (Mt. 26:36–46). Jesus prayed with tears in his eyes and anguish in his soul (Heb. 5:7) but these emotions did not stop him seeking the face of his Father wholeheartedly. That evening he was under severe stress: lonely – the disciples had fallen asleep – tired, facing torture and death, but this never interrupted the precious fellowship, the constant spiritual flow, with the Father. In fact, the words of Jesus in Gethsemane gave us a masterpiece in prayer. Jesus needed to cry: he was deeply anxious. That didn't make him a sinner – depression of itself is not a sin. His tears while praying did not make him less spiritual but more fully human. His need to pour out all the anguish in his heart showed he truly 'has been tempted in every way, just as we are – yet was without sin' (Heb. 4:15). The words of Pilate some hours later – 'Ecce homo', 'Behold the Man' – were a memorable summary of our Lord's essence: fully God and fully Man. Yet this perfection did not remove the influence of certain emotions and feelings from his life.

I shall return to this example of Jesus later, because I feel that it is of fundamental importance today, in view of the powerful resurgence of age-old neoplatonist thought patterns that are dressed up as super-spirituality. For the moment, though, we may conclude that the believer is a unity of these three dimensions, and that none of the three is superior to the others, and that none can be isolated from the others. This is the concept of man that we find in the Scriptures; biblical anthropology is holistic, integrated and, consequently, so is the Bible's concept of the Christian life, including prayer. No one can set aside their state of mind, their emotions or their circumstances before coming to God in prayer.

Therefore, the influences upon our prayer life that come from our inner structure, from our essential make-up as human beings, are realities with which we must come to terms. These influences are not negative in themselves, nor should we always see them as limitations. Undoubtedly at times they are a thorn in the flesh, preventing us from praying as we would like. But we should bear in mind from the outset that, far from being obstacles, it is our temperament, our personality and our circumstances that give our spiritual life its distinctive quality. I might sum up this idea with a paraphrase of the famous dictum of the Spanish philosopher Ortega y Gasset that 'my prayer is me and my circumstances'. Psychological factors exercise a partial and limited – but all the same, powerful – influence on our prayer life. We must accept this reality as one of the spheres where the Trinity works, moulding and shaping us (Phil. 1:6).

Let us see how these influences actually operate. I shall begin with some considerations concerning temperament.

Temperament

Temperament is the most constitutional – or genetic – part of our character. It is the aspect of our personality that is mainly determined by biological factors: we are born with certain tendencies. Freedman and Kaplan's glossary defines it as 'the intrinsic, constitutional propensity to react in a given manner to different stimuli'.[1] As a general rule, it is accepted that there is an undeniable genetic, hereditary component, that cannot be changed, in the formation of the temperament.

How does this show itself? For example, if your father tends to be anxious – anxiety is partly of the temperament – then you are also likely to be anxious. If both your father and your mother are anxious, then you are almost bound to be an anxious person. The same is true of the other features of our temperament. It is very much determined by genetics: we can change it but only to a certain extent. There are some elements we cannot change.

There are many and varied classifications of the temperament. Most of them are useful in that they highlight predetermined aspects of the person. The typology put forward by Hippocrates, for example, despite its antiquity, still enjoys widespread acceptance, especially in evangelical circles. The work done by the Norwegian theologian Hallesby in his brief but very readable booklet (now out of print) *Your Temperament and your faith in God*[2] is an admirable example. Tim La Haye follows the same pattern laid down by Hippocrates in his book *Spirit-Controlled Temperaments*.[3] The four-fold classification: melancholic, choleric, sanguine and phlegmatic, is now deeply rooted in popular psychology, and I believe that such wide acceptance comes from its very practical applications.

For our present purposes, however, I have preferred a less well-known, but more modern, classification: that of the Swiss psychiatrist, Karl Gustav Jung.[4] Jung is a somewhat controversial thinker, both in professional and in Christian circles (he was the first 'heretic' to deviate from Freudian orthodoxy). The reasons for objecting, from a Christian viewpoint, to some aspects of his work will be put forward in chapter 5. But Jung has left us many useful and enriching insights into the human mind. We cannot write off all his work simply because we do not share some of his views. His classification of people according to their psychological type is one of these insights and is worthy of our respect and appreciation. I have chosen his typology because it emphasises flexibility and also a certain possibility of change. As I have said, some people are reluctant to use this kind of typology because it is rigid and labels people in closed boxes. This is not the case with Jung's classification, which shows a wide range of functioning, according to our circumstances and situations. We should remember that every human being is unique and, therefore, in a strict sense classifications are always somewhat relative. Jung's classification revolves around two fundamental axes:

- According to one's general attitude: introversion – extroversion:
- According to one's predominant psychological function: four psychological types.

Introversion and extroversion

Jung divides human beings into two main types: those whose general attitudes, interests and energy are directed outwards are extrovert: those whose general attitudes are directed inwards are introvert. These two attitudes are not primarily the result of the social climate or education: they are rather spontaneous, automatic ways of reacting – temperamental features which are biologically conditioned.

Nevertheless, it must be stressed that it is not a question of a choice between one and the other: a person is not either introvert or extrovert. Temperament is rather a continuum along which everybody can situate themselves. One person might be 60% extrovert and 40% introvert: for someone else the proportion will be different. A certain degree of change from one attitude to another is possible and sometimes even desirable. The person who will suffer is one who is 80% one and 20% the other, or even 90% one and 10% the other. The closer we are to the balance of 50% extrovert and 50% introvert, the better.

In fact, every human being potentially possesses both possibilities. We all go through periods of our lives when we have a tendency towards introversion, adolescence for example. Consequently, there can be fluctuations in these basic attitudes. In spite of that, however, one of the two attitudes will always be predominant; one will react in a more spontaneous, automatic way than the other. For example, an introvert is a person who wishes they could speak more in the company of others, while an extrovert will repent of how much they have spoken. An introvert's brain works much quicker than their tongue: an extrovert is the opposite.

In introversion, the person's vital energy is directed inwards. They will be shy, lacking in fluency and adaptability in their relationships. Introverts need a lot of privacy. They are comfortable alone: people – especially crowds – tire them. They prefer activities that involve few or no other people. This doesn't mean that they don't like being with others. Introverts enjoy interacting with some people but it drains their emotional energy. For this reason they need to find quietness to 'recharge their batteries'. An introvert is likely to return home exhausted after a party! Meditation and introspection come naturally to them, and their inner life is their main source of delight. Far more interested in ideas than in things, they enjoy reading books and meditating on the word of God. Given their rich inner life, they inhabit their dreams, their speculations, their own private universe. To look deeply into the affairs of the soul will be far easier for an introvert than an extrovert. Consequently, they do not find it difficult to cultivate a fairly regular prayer life.

Introverts prefer praying in solitude; they may feel uncomfortable in prayer meetings where there is a more extrovert expression of emotions. Their prayer is born from their remarkable depth of feeling and thought, not so much from the immediate stimuli around. If they have to pray out loud, and this can be torture to them, they become more nervous than the extrovert and pray shorter prayers, but the substance of their prayer shows how much an introvert may feel inside. Although they do not like showing their emotions, they do have fire in their hearts. In summary, their spirituality is a rich treasure for the church in a society that is increasingly attracted by superficiality and sensationalism. We need introverts in our churches because they enrich our spiritual lives – particularly our prayer lives.

In the case of extroversion, on the other hand, the person's psychological energy is directed outwards. The extrovert is a sociable person, adapting easily to their environment and relating effortlessly to the outside world. Their interests are not centred on their own private universe but around people and things. They are, by nature, open to others, and one of their worst enemies is loneliness. Their need for sociability is striking: an extrovert becomes more and more alive as a party continues! They 'recharge their batteries' from their interaction with others. Unlike the introvert, they experience quietness or solitude almost as a punishment. Having to stay at home alone for a long time is uncomfortable; they need to go out and it doesn't matter where! They like outdoor activities, preferably with others, rather than indoor. They need as much contact with others as they can get.

Extroverts are people with attractive personalities at first sight, while the attractions of an introvert become apparent as one gets to know them. Extroverts and introverts are naturally attracted to each other. You will find more couples who complement each other than those that bring sim-

ilar temperaments together, because those of similar temperaments don't attract each other in the same way.

The extrovert's natural tendency is towards action
rather than meditation: they will be the ones doing things
in the church, because they need to be active all the time.
Consequently, they find it difficult to maintain a regular
prayer life. The more extrovert a person is, the more difficult they find it to pray and to concentrate while praying
– too much to do! Introverts, on the other hand, are much
more methodical and will set time apart. Extroverts find
difficulty in cultivating their inner life, which suffers in
consequence. Their thoughts and feelings flow spontaneously outwards, so beginning to pray is rather like having to make an enormous leap, and therefore they usually
choose praying with others rather than privately. Prayer
meetings give them the opportunity to relate with others,
which is precisely the source of energy they need to start
praying. Once they are in the atmosphere of a group, they
enjoy participation; this community flavour is just the
kind of stimulus they need to warm them up spiritually.
When they pray in solitude, they do so briefly and will not
come out very inspired or spiritually high. They're not
energized by quiet reflection but by what's going on
around them. For them, prayer is linked with service and
action. The focus of their requests is the needs of the world
rather than the inner world, unlike the introvert.

So if you identify with both – congratulations: the
more balance there is in temperamental matters, the better. Now let us move on to Jung's second criterion:

The psychological functions

In order to adapt to the outside world and to themselves, every individual is endowed with four main

functions: thought, feeling, sensation and intuition. These functions, just like the two attitudes outlined above, are inborn. Every human being possesses all four of them, but in differing degrees of development. As a rule, one of them will be more highly developed than the other three: this is known as the principal function and is the one that reacts most spontaneously. Another acts in second place as an auxiliary function. The third and fourth are more or less unconscious and rudimentary.

As with introversion/extroversion, the four psychological functions are grouped on axes; there are two axes: the thinking/feeling axis and the sensation/intuitive axis. The auxiliary function cannot belong to the same axis – so it is not possible to have thinking as your main function and feeling as your auxiliary, and so on. Again, the optimum state is to be balanced on these axes – to be as close to 50% one and 50% the other.

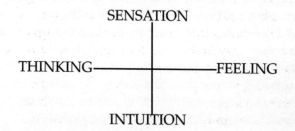

People are, therefore, one of eight types – with the predominant function first and auxiliary second.

The eight groupings are :
Thinking/intuitive
Thinking/sensation
Feeling/intuitive
Feeling/sensation
Sensation/thinking

Sensation/feeling
Intuitive/thinking
Intuitive/feeling

These eight groupings are then doubled by the addition
of the extroversion or introversion axis to each one. As a
matter of fact, this classification is also used in other
areas, such as marriage counselling and professional-
vocational orientation.

Particular professions that might be suited to some of
these types include:

Sensation/thinking – introvert: art collector, good sup-
    ervisors, co-ordinators.
Feeling/sensation – extrovert: public relations, excellent
    party host, professions requiring service to others.
Thinking/sensation – extrovert: lawyer, professions
    requiring a good sense of responsibility.
Sensation/thinking – extrovert: businessman, good
    leaders.
Feeling/intuitive – introvert: musician, medical doctor,
    psychologist, psychiatrist.
Intuitive/feeling – extrovert: excellent communicators,
    commercial and mass media professions.
Thinking/intuitive – introvert: researcher, scientist,
    engineer.

According to Jung, many disorders of the psyche result
from an imbalance among these four functions. If one of
them is excessively developed, at the expense of the
other three, a person will experience emotional
upheaval. Consequently, the ideal state would be that of
perfect balance among all four; but it is hard to find a
person with the four functions – thought, sensation,

intuition and feeling – all in an equal state of development.

Nevertheless, it is useful to know that we can stimulate the development of the less developed functions; their state is not static and irreversible, a legacy that we have received and must fatalistically come to terms with. One of the keys to the maturing of the individual, according to Jung, is the stimulation of the less developed functions. He calls this process individuation.

Let us take the example of a person who is very much a thinking type, and who hasn't developed their capacity to express emotions at all. This is quite common in families where cold and distant parents did not encourage but rather repressed all that had to do with feelings. A thinking type person is not condemned to be this way all their life: they can stimulate the growth of the less developed function – feeling – by a process which requires practice and effort. In this process the main function should be maintained and respected as such. Our emotional life will actually be more harmonious and happier when we lean on our main function. It is the most natural, the one that helps us adapt to the world in a spontaneous way. Not leaning on our main function can lead to emotional problems. We cannot pretend to be what we are not endowed to be.

Having this in mind, how can we improve those functions which are rudimentary? These are some basic suggestions for change:

- Identify and be aware of your least developed function.
- Notice its main features, how it reacts.
- Think of someone for whom it is the main function. Imagine their reactions and attitudes.
- Start training this function in the same way you would learn a foreign language – by practising it a lot.

The more you repeat certain reactions, the easier and more natural they will become.

● Circumstances are a great help in this process of change. This is especially true with personal relationships. The more intimate a relationship, the greater are the possibilities or influence and therefore of change.

● Remember however that this can also happen in a negative way – that is going away from the desired balance of 50/50.

After this general introduction, we are ready to consider how these types influence our prayer lives. We will look more closely at the four functions that determine psychological types. Remember that when I talk about a particular psychological function, I am referring to a person's principle function, the way they most naturally react. This does not mean they do not possess the other functions but these are less developed.

The Thinking Type

In thinking types, logic prevails over feeling, the objective over the subjective. Reason is their guide in every situation. The first question to occur to them about any given circumstance is: 'What does this mean?' They do have feelings, but these are not their first tools to approach reality. This can be a problem in many of their relationships, especially marriage. Remember, opposites attract, and feeling types are attracted by thinking types, and vice versa. While thinking types may not be intellectuals in the usual sense, they enjoy thinking. They proceed by logical deduction and they feel at home with whatever implies reflection. They search for truth and meaning. For them, principles are more important than emotions, therefore things are not pleasant or unpleasant, attractive or ugly, but true or false, logical or illogical. They love books and take enormous pleasure in the world of ideas. They are always classifying and analysing: they often have collections, such as stamps or butterflies, and are very methodical. We could say that their head is the most developed part of them, much more so than their heart

In extreme cases, they may be insensitive people. They are sometimes oblivious to the emotional needs and moods of others; gauche when it comes to discerning the subtle variations of the heart. An extreme illustration of this is the man of letters and ideas living in his ivory tower. Given this deficit in the emotional sphere, another of the dangers faced by this type is intolerance: they can be too rigid, incapable of accepting the idiosyncrasies or opinions of others. They should be on their guard against this tendency to dogmatism, together with their excessively rationalistic mentality. They must ensure that their head does not grow out of proportion with their heart, remembering the perfect balance between truth and life that was characteristic of Jesus. They should cultivate their feelings and accept those of other people. The fact of thinking more than other people does not confer a greater degree of spirituality on anyone.

Prayer is, for them, a mental activity, performed more with the head than with the heart. They come to God with a rational mentality, and what matters for them when they pray is not so much the possibility of feeling God but the rush of new spiritual ideas that flow into their minds. They probably even use a notebook and jot down these ideas as they occur. Some of them might have a devotional diary which proves to be of great benefit to them. Other psychological types, the feeling type, for example, would be scandalized by this approach!

How can something so full of emotion as prayer be done with pencil and paper?

As a rule, thinking types will find it more difficult than others to get down to praying, because prayer implies relationship; it is an expression of feelings, and this is not easy for them. They find relationships demanding; more so if they are introverts. 'I would find it much easier to write God a letter,' expresses this difficulty. They enjoy the theological perspectives of prayer but not the expression of emotion while praying. Since prayer does not come naturally to them, the 'thinking' type needs to make a particular effort to start it. More than any of the others, they will need to find adequate stimuli to help them begin to pray. In this respect, community prayer might be a great encouragement to them. The prayer life of the local church is an indispensable stimulus for every believer, but it is much more so for these people.

The thinking types are usually disciplined and methodical. They like order, and make excellent prayer partners. They often use prayer lists. But they are not so good at adoration and worship. Before praying, they prefer to have an objective basis, and often find their inspiration in a text of Scripture. They find it difficult, however, to maintain the devotional quality of their meditation. Given their natural tendency to intellectualise everything, they find themselves – without realizing it – preparing sermons or analysing the exegesis of the text, though in the first place they came to it in a spirit of devotion. In any case, the reading of Scripture will give them a more solid foundation on which to base their reflections about God. Their meditation will be more a search for new ideas, the light that flows from logic, from coherence of argument.

Spiritual self-analysis will be an essential feature of this person's relationship with God. The positive upshot of this is their remarkable capacity for self-criticism and confession. On the other hand, there is a danger that too much introspection might turn them into 'spiritual hypochondriacs', with a disproportionate concern for their spiritual health. In their prayers, the main concern of these believers will be for justice and truth: they find themselves especially attracted to the Beatitudes. Their logical structure, their interconnectedness, like the links of a chain, and their emphasis on truth, all strike a chord with their temperament. This characteristic makes them excellent intercessors on behalf of people or situations in the world.

The attitude of the 'thinking' type could be summed up in the following terms: 'meditating on God's word is no problem for me. I enjoy that immensely. But I find it difficult to feel God's presence when I pray. Curiously enough, if I manage to "connect" with the Lord, then my prayer is intense.'

In general, their spiritual life is marked by stability, without many ups or downs. They may be dry sometimes, but even in periods of spiritual dryness, they are able to trust God and find streams of water in the desert. This firmness in their faith makes them a bulwark in the church, as they can lead and encourage others in times of difficulty. Martin Luther, the great reformer, and especially the apostle Paul are both good examples of this type of Christian. Paul also reminds us of the very desirable possibility of having these temperament traits in balance. His feeling function was also highly developed: the tender and encouraging chapter of 1 Thessalonians chapter 2 is a striking example of how you can be a good thinker and a caring pastor at the same time.

The Feeling Type

Feeling is the emotion that conveys to us the value of things. The feeling type approaches reality influenced by the question: do I like this or not? Do I feel attracted or repelled? They are not so concerned about truth or falsehood, or logic, as thinking types are. They prefer deciding on the basis of personal impact: principles are secondary. Women are often feeling types, as are artists, musicians, poets and other creative people. They are tender, intimate people with a remarkable capacity for giving warmth and affection. Personal relationships, especially those that require self-giving are their strong point. They have a greatly developed gift that we could call 'the sense of the person', seeing each human being as a creature of precious value – never an object. Their speciality is treating people as real people. If they met you after a five year interval, they would remember you and would remember your name. The thinking type would have forgotten you. And when you were talking to the thinking type, many of them would not have looked into your eyes – but they would have been interested in your ideas. Thinking types often become scientists, philosophers or political leaders, while feeling types can be found in all the caring professions – nurses, teachers, psychologists, doctors and social workers and also often become writers.

If the head predominates with the thinking type, with the feeling type the heart is most important, and we should never say that one is superior to the other. They are different and, consequently, complementary. Mutual acceptance is again needed here. The feeling person will sometimes claim that thinking people are 'cold', 'have ice in their veins' and are 'heartless'. On the other hand, they will be accused by the thinking types of being illogical, too emotional and soft-hearted. But these reproaches will lead nowhere in our relationships. We have to learn to identify the negative aspects in our neighbour's temperament, not in order to criticize them, but to promote the acceptance of our diversity. One of the most beautiful things we find in God's creation is variety. The main reason for understanding the way we are, our temperament and personality, is not to make us feel better but to make real improvements in our relationships, both with God and with our brothers and sisters.

One observation is necessary here. The idea that the feeling types are more emotional than the thinking people is not an accurate one. Both types can react emotionally with similar intensity. The difference lies in the expression of feelings: feeling types tend to be more able to communicate such feelings, they are able to warm others up, whereas the thinking person is usually more reserved in expressing their emotions. The feeling person often enjoys the open show of feelings (especially extrovert feelings), whereas this makes the thinking type somewhat embarrassed.

Consequently, the prayer life of the feeling type will possess all the features of a warm personal relationship. They will have no difficulty in feeling God as a sensitive friend and as a loving Father. His most appealing attributes, to them, will be his kindness and mercy. They give more importance to values and ideals than to knowledge. They will look for inspiration in a sermon, while the thinking type will want sound theology and relevant application. Feeling types like symbols and metaphors, and one of the texts that attracts them the most is that of the Good Shepherd (Jn. 10), who watches over and cares for the sheep with profound love. For the feeling type, God is my Father, Abba. For the thinking type, God is the first person of the Trinity.

Feeling types are usually concerned about concrete situations of injustice and social need. They are naturally sympathetic to the outcasts in society: the orphans, the poor or deprived, and those in prison. They have a special discernment of the needs of their neighbours and their capacity to care for others and to offer themselves to the Lord is remarkable. They are almost always ready to be 'Good Samaritans' – we need feeling types in our churches.

A longing for intimacy with God is the distinguishing feature of the feeling type's prayer life. Of all the types, they are the best equipped to feel the presence of the Lord as a lover and to understand faith as a love relationship (see chapter 3). Their emphasis on the personal and the immediate accounts for their emphasising God's closeness instead of God's transcendence. For them, formal prayer, the practice of setting aside a specific time to pray is not difficult when they understand it as a personal appointment with 'my God'. But this task is not always easy for them because they lack the self-discipline of other types (e.g., the thinking type) and they need strong emotional motivation.

The feeling dimension enables them to see Christ and the Holy Spirit as living persons, as alive and real as the human beings around them. For this very reason, when their capacity to feel is decreased – for example, by depression or tiredness – God or Christ seem very far away. Therefore, the main danger here is the excessive subjectivism in their prayer life. 'When I feel that God is near, my faith is strong. If he feels far away, my faith doesn't work and I'm a hypocrite.' People who belong to this group must learn to explore more objective dimensions of prayer: intercession and supplication, for example.

We find good examples of this type in the Bible. Jeremiah, the sensitive prophet, whose personal relationship with God is thoroughly considered in chapter 2. Barnabas, one of the key leaders in the early church, whose name means 'son of encouragement', is another; as is Mary, sister of Lazarus, who chose 'the good part' – her close spiritual relationship with Jesus. These and many other biblical examples show us how God used and still uses very different kinds of people to build his church.

The Intuitive Type

Intuitive types see the possibilities of a person, thing or situation beyond what is apparent on the surface. They discern what lies hidden, anticipating possibilities. This kind of person, then, is a visionary in the best sense of the word. (We should bear in mind that, etymologically, the meaning of the original word in Latin – *intueri* – means to contemplate.) These people are innovators, pioneers; they are initiators – though not the followers – of thoughts and actions. One might say that the intuitive type is the spark that lights the fire, but not the fuel that keeps it burning. They are almost always oriented toward the future, to what lies beyond. The present, the here and now, seems prosaic to them. They are attracted by the unknown, by what is new. They get enthusiastic about an idea but often leave many tasks unfinished because they are usually lacking in realism. Prototypes of extreme intuition might be inventors and explorers. Their minds are full of visions and projects. They are idealists, but not realists. Evangelists and missionaries are often intuitive type – David Livingstone was probably an intuitive.

An interesting feature of the intuitive type in comparison with other types, is their spontaneous spirituality, a natural mysticism – which is not necessarily Christian.

Of all the types they are the best equipped to perceive religious reality; they have an innate sensitivity to spiritual things; we could almost say that we are dealing with a highly developed religious instinct, a temperamental spirituality. A patient once said to me, 'I am spiritual by nature; the eternal and transcendental appeal to me; they attract me spontaneously; I feel them inside me without having to make any effort.' This is a precise illustration of the kind of feature we are dealing with.

It goes without saying that this natural religiousness is not the same as faith in the biblical sense. But it must be admitted that the intuitive type will be more open to spiritual realities than, for example, the sensation type who is, by nature, much more attracted to concrete realities.

For these reasons, they find it easier to enter the presence of God in prayer, particularly if they are introverts. By nature, intuitive types quickly and easily cross the threshold from their own inner world to the divine, because both worlds are very close to them. The path they must follow in order to begin to pray is very short, much shorter than for both the thinking and sensation types – especially if they are extrovert.

Their prayers, especially in the case of introvert intuition types, come very close to the mystic idea of prayer. As has been pointed out already, their reality is made up of visions, inspirations and rich images. They greatly value God as Spirit and their souls are attracted to the mystery of God. Intuitive types are absorbed in their inner world which they experience as easily as the sensation type experiences the outer world. Theresa of Avila, St John of the Cross and other mystics could be considered prototypes of this group. Symbols have an important role in the prayers of intuitive people; and the gospel of John and the book of Revelation often figure among their favourites. The gospel writer John was an intuitive and probably an introvert – otherwise why would God have chosen him to write the gospel of John and Revelation? John is the prototype of the intuitive visionary.

An intuitive's prayer life will therefore centre around the mystical, rather than the concrete. The intuitive type is capable of imagining heaven with extraordinary richness; but they find it much more difficult to pray for the immediate needs of their local church. They might be deeply moved when they take part in Holy Communion, as they imagine the suffering of Christ; but they have difficulty in identifying with their own brothers and sisters who are being unjustly persecuted in another country. They are not good at saying 'thank you' or praying for others, and do not make good intercessors. Sometimes they may not feel the need for a specific prayer time. Wanting their prayer time to be purely spontaneous, and only praying when they feel like it, when they have the inspiration or the vision, they may end up without discipline in their prayer lives. They must be alert to this danger.

The most natural way for intuitive types to meditate tends to be abstract, without specific content, with all the dangers that this implies. This is especially true today, when postmodernism is greatly influencing spirituality. Its emphasis is more on a shallow spirituality, empty of content, so light that it is mere subjectivism. A spirituality that is without God and without beliefs may be a good self-relaxation exercise, but it has nothing to do with the Christian concept of prayer and meditation. Another danger that intuitives face lies in their tend-ency toward purely contemplative and non-verbal prayer, toward ecstasy, toward mystical 'union with God', at the expense of prayer's other important ingredients.

Intuitive types shun methods; freedom in prayer is vital to them because it enables them to immerse themselves in the 'inward voyage of the soul', along unknown, unexplored spiritual paths, to accede to the mystery of God in an experimental manner. To this end, they might be inclined to use ready-made prayers, or set phrases, repeating them in routine fashion until they achieve the state of mind required for them to commence their 'trip'.

In any case, the intuitive type is the most vulnerable to the kind of dangers explained in fuller detail in chapter 5, dangers which are now threatening the basics of biblical spirituality:

- A false concept of spirituality; false in the sense that it is more platonic than biblical. Super-spirituality is just a short step away from pseudo-spirituality.
- A prayer life that is more an exercise in psychological catharsis, a personal self-expression rather than a relationship with the God of the Bible.
- Surrender to the mysterious, hidden paths of the spirit, which leaves us open to the influences of the evil one, as has been acknowledged by experts in the 'inner journey'.
- A subtle flirting with Eastern religion. In practice, indulging in contemplative prayer can become a kind of mantra,[5] even though we may not be conscious of the fact. But ignorance does not protect us from a practice that is much closer to transcendental meditation than Christian meditation.

The intuitive type should make sure that their feet are on the ground. If they really want their prayer life to be an experience of the love of Christ, they must 'come down' to earthly reality; they cannot always be praying in celestial regions. They must cultivate intercessory prayer for concrete needs. They must centre their meditation on the word of God, 'on the law of the Lord', rather than letting their minds wander around the cosmic infinite. In short, they must learn to pray in the midst of problems and the tribulations of this world, because that was how our Master prayed. There are subtle forms of monasticism which enable us to detach ourselves from this world without physically entering into any kind of monastery. We must be on our guard in case something that is apparently very spiritual becomes a form of escapism. The Lord does not want us to be 'of the world', but he does want us to be 'in the world'. A balanced biblical spirituality requires having one foot in heaven, but the other on earth. Having both feet on earth can be mere humanism, but if both are in heaven, this can become a form of escapism.

We need intuitive types in the church because their vision of the future and their rich spirituality are invaluable gifts in a time of materialism. The history of the church is greatly indebted to their contributions which have been milestones in the growth of the body of Christ.

The Sensation Type

The sensation type registers everything around him – everything is perception. The forefront of their activity is not the head (thinking type), nor the heart (feeling type), nor contemplation (intuitive type), but the senses. They incessantly see, hear, touch. Everything that can be perceived matters to this person: colours, flavours, shapes, all practical details. They are characterized by their spontaneity. Their feelings are aroused easily; they are effusive. They might feel let down by God, and even be angry with him, but they get over it quickly. Due to their extraordinary capacity for perception, they pick up and intensely feel an entire host of impressions. They have a very practical sense of reality, and are excellent housewives or househusbands. They express themselves in a very spontaneous way – almost like children – and they find it difficult to concentrate on abstract realities. Nonetheless, they have a strong sense of responsibility and you can trust them fully in administrative affairs. They are good organisers and can take care of the smallest detail with great efficiency. They are very faithful in their relationships.

Sensation types do not find it enormously difficult to relate to God. They talk to him as if they were talking to a friend, but with one particular distinguishing feature: their prayers are spontaneous. An adequate external stimulus will move them to 'informal' prayer. Thus, a sunset, a landscape, an aesthetically beautiful scene, will be enough to make them break out in spontaneous praise to the Lord. God is immediate to them, but they do not find it easy to pray in any formal, structured sense. We should bear in mind, however, this extraordinary capacity for impromptu, spontaneous prayer and worship which is also necessary in the church. There is no one to compare with them in that respect.

Their prayers tend to be characterized by simple thoughts. They are direct and rather naïve. We might say that they approach God with the soul of a child. They may have an idea of God which is incomplete because they are not very fond of in-depth Bible teaching. Superficiality in their spiritual life can be one of their weak points, unless they have 'thinking' as their auxiliary function. They live in the present moment, not the future, and their prayer life seems to be mainly centred around the here and now. They have a good capacity to be in touch with real situations; this is why they like detail and specifics when prayer requests are given. When they are alone, they cannot pray for long: a sensation type will not pray for more than a few minutes, especially not the extrovert sensation type, whereas an intuitive type can pray for very long periods. The feeling type would come in between these two extremes, and a thinking type, armed with a notebook, will also pray for a long time.

Given their reliance on external circumstances, the sensation type may suffer from frequent ups and downs. A small problem or tension can plunge them into a depression of the same intensity as the euphoria that might have characterized them a moment before. However, unlike the feeling type, their 'downs' are very short and they quickly recover their natural enjoyment of life. They are upset by changes and like stable customs which might lead to rigidity, perhaps even to an extreme. They are not much concerned with the intellectual abstractions of the thinking type, nor the mystical impulses of the intuitive type

Their main difficulty lies in concentration while praying. This is understandable because their minds are hyperactive, like Martha, Mary's sister, who was 'worried and upset about many things'. This prevents them being able to stop and find the inner quietness that prayer needs. On the other hand, as solemnity, rituals and forms of worship are very important to them, the sensation type will find it much easier to pray in community; of all the types, they are the most in need of the stimulus of fellowship with their brothers and sisters in order to pray – particularly if they are extroverts. So, prayer in the church will come much more easily to them than private prayer at home, and they share this characteristic with the thinking type, especially the extrovert.

The apostle Peter is a good example of this type, although he also had a developed thinking function. His life and character show us how God uses even our weaknesses to work out his purposes. I am sure Peter often wished for a quieter introvert temperament, but Pentecost with its fullness of the Holy Spirit did not change the basic structure of his temperament. On the other hand, if God had endowed Peter with specific gifts and talents, they were closely related to his character. When God calls us to a task, he always equips us with the most suitable and necessary resources, including our temperament and personality – whether we like them or not!

We must remember that everyone has two developed functions: the principle function and the auxiliary. For this reason, you will see yourself reflected in more than one of the types. If you see yourself in all four, this is a good sign; it shows that your psychological functions are moving towards a harmonious balance, which means that you are on the way toward maturity.

So much for Jung's basic scheme and our particular application of it to prayer. In the next chapter I shall explore these concepts further and see how they apply to the flow and content of prayer. First, however, let us look at a few of the implications.

Conclusions

From all that we have been looking at so far, we must retain whatever is of greatest use to us for our Christian lives. These psychological descriptions are not meant to serve merely academic ends. I have gone into considerable depth in order to help the believer to understand three fundamental realities:

We must accept one another

We are all very different from one another. The coming together of genetic, biographical and circumstantial factors makes each individual a little universe that is very different from all the others. This is reflected in the way in which we understand and live out our faith. These differences can, at times, be so enormous that we stand at opposite poles from each other, even in spiritual matters. Our human tendency is to reject behavioural patterns and temperaments that are different from our own. By nature we can be rather rigid and intolerant, approaching our neighbour in a judicial frame of mind, and, even without realizing it, we would like to turn others into a 'photocopy' of ourselves.

For this reason we must understand that many of these differences do not stem from a greater or lesser amount of faith but are the result of the way we are. God has given the intuitive type an enormous capacity for mysticism. But the latter should not then condemn the sensation type as superficial and simplistic because their prayers are briefer and more spontaneous. In the same way, the sensation type must not accuse the intuitive of always having their head in the clouds. The thinking type must not complain that the feeling type is hypersensitive, all heart and no head. The feeling type should not reject the thinking type as just cold intellect. And we could go on with our list of accusations which are, sadly enough, by no means infrequent among believers.

We are different and we must respect one another. There is no type of spirituality that, from the temperamental point of view, is superior to any other type. No one has the monopoly on prayer! The church is a many dimensional body, with a multitude of differences among its members. One of these differences is the tem-

peramental one. The unity of the church does not
depend on the uniformity of its members. We should
remember the words of C.S. Lewis exhorting us to tolerance within the Christian church. He describes
Christianity as 'more like a hall out of which doors open
into several rooms … When you have reached your own
room, be kind to those who have chosen different doors
and to those who are still in the hall.'[6]

What is true of individuals is also true, to a certain
degree, of churches and even denominations. Some
churches are thinking churches, while others are feeling
or sensation churches. The ideal church, perfectly balanced in all its functions, does not exist because every
church is the mirror of its members. Therefore, we
should accept each other, enrich each other, help each
other and practice the least developed area in our particular church. The metaphor of the church as a body is
very meaningful and it reflects the features which are
essential for the functioning of the body: unity, balance
and diversity. Actually it is remarkable to discover that
this is exactly how the Trinity works. How many problems and sadness could have been avoided if the church
had learnt that division, extremism and intolerance are
favourite tools of the devil to destroy the body.

We must accept ourselves

Every temperament has its good side and its dark side.
Many believers long to be different from what they are.
They compare themselves with their brothers and sisters
within the church or with members of their own family
and they are envious of other people's personalities. We
must remember that Jesus did not change the temperaments of the disciples after he had called them, not even
after Pentecost. As I said before, Peter, for example, con-

tinued to be spontaneous and impulsive, the prototype of the sensation type; the Holy Spirit did not alter his basic temper but he did polish it and mould it. Peter did not cut any more ears off after Pentecost, but he did not cease to be spontaneous and direct. The weaknesses of our temperament can be controlled by the action of the Holy Spirit so that it does not lead us to sin. But, it would be futile to expect a drastic change in the genetic makeup of our person.

As we have seen, there is no temperament that is better than any other. All of them have admirable features when viewed from a divine perspective. The Lord can use each of us just as we are, with all our virtues and defects, and he often uses us not so much in spite of our weaknesses as through them. The words of the Lord to the apostle Paul, as recorded in 2 Corinthians 12:9, are conclusive: 'My grace is sufficient for you, for my power is made perfect in weakness.' This is God's reply to Paul's intense desire to be rid of his thorn in the flesh. If God accepts us as we are, why can we not accept ourselves? We must come to terms with the limitations that our temperament imposes on our life of faith in general, and on our prayers in particular, except when sin is involved. Our temperament is not our enemy but our ally. We are not required to like our temperament, but to work through it for God's glory in our lives.

We need to cultivate a temperamental balance

Having said that, we must not fall into false indulgence or passivity. We must cultivate our least developed features, our most rudimentary psychological function, by practising it, especially if it is affecting our spiritual lives. As I pointed out before, it is a matter of training. This will enable us progressively to approach a state of balance among the principle function and the shadows (less developed functions). This in turn will lead to a better relationship with our neighbour, with ourselves and with the Lord.

Jesus, the perfect man, held all four functions in perfect balance. He has been the only human being to hold them in harmony.[7] For this reason, we must not resign ourselves to a state of imbalance in our temperament, because our aim is to become more and more like Christ. Let us open ourselves up to the influence of the Holy Spirit and let the Supreme Potter mould us, but let us not forget that we are vessels of clay and not of silver or gold.

In summary, it is reassuring to reach the conclusion that temperament is the seal that stamps an individual uniqueness in our relationship with God. Our temperamental code admits no possibility of being copied. Therefore, just as no two human beings have the same fingerprints, neither will two believers have an identical spiritual experience. This personal and distinctive seal of our faith, so deeply grafted into our temperaments, constitutes one of the most precious possessions in the life of each believer.

> If I do not want what you want, please try not to tell me that my want is wrong.
>
> Or if I believe other than you, at least pause before you correct my view.
>
> Or if my emotion is less than yours, or more, given the same circumstances, try not to ask me to feel more strongly or weakly.
>
> Or yet if I act, or fail to act, in the manner of your design for action, let me be.
>
> I do not, for the moment at least, ask you to understand me. That will come only when you are willing to give up changing me into a copy of you.[8]

1 Freedman & Kaplan, *Comprehensive Textbook of Psychiatry* (Baltimore: William and Wilkins, 1980), p3360

2 O. Hallesby, *Your temperament and your faith in God* (Minneapolis: Augsburg Publishing House, 1972)

3 T. La Haye, *Spirit-Controlled Temperaments*

4 K.G. Jung, *Tipos Psicologicos* (Barcelona: Edhasa Editorial, 1994)

5 *Mantra* is the name given to a sacred utterance considered to possess supernatural power. Mantras are used as ritual and mechanical repetitions to concentrate the mind, especially in Brahmanism

6 C.S. Lewis, *Mere Christianity*, Preface (London: Fontana, 1972) p12

7 J. Sandford, *The Kingdom Within* (London: Paulist Press, 1970)

8 D. Keirsey & M. Bates, *Please Understand Me* (Del Mar, California: Prometheus Nemesis Books, 1978), p1

Chapter 2

OVERCOMING THE DIFFICULTIES

Emotional problems and prayer

So far we have considered the influence of the first factor: temperament, realizing that we are born with a predisposition to react in a certain way and that this affects our prayer life. Some pray one way, others another. The same could be said of our different approaches to spirituality or the way we understand faith.

We saw how different temperaments respond to different styles of prayer and how enriching these different flavours can become in our individual as well as our corporate Christian life. We should not try to force our brothers and sisters into a particular form of praying, but respect and accept them. Nor should we let these different flavours divide us; they can be very enriching.

Now we are going to consider a second fundamental component in our personality: all that is mainly the result of our biography, our past memories. It is the end product of what we have done and what we have had done to us, and comes together with another essential element in our personality: our unconscious. These two factors, our past and our unconscious, are inseparably bound up with each other. We must begin by coming to terms, not only with their existence, but also with the extent of their influence. Remember that temperament is more genetic; it is the biological part of our personality, to do with the raw materials that we were born with. Now let us see what has happened to and what we have done with those raw materials since birth. Our past, and the deposit of experience stored up in our subconscious, will be powerful forces in our lives as a whole, and therefore in our spiritual lives. But this influence does not mean that our responsibility is diminished, as the extreme deterministic position that we have briefly considered would maintain. We should not delude ourselves into thinking that these factors do not affect us, but likewise we must not feel that we are mere victims of their influence.

Let us start by clarifying a practical point which is sometimes misunderstood by those who are young in the faith. Some believers think that upon conversion, we can start from scratch in every area of our lives. It is as if the Holy Spirit cleans the slate of our personalities instantaneously, wiping off everything that corresponds to our past. This way of thinking reflects more an urgent emotional desire for change than a mature longing for Christ's likeness; the person longs to be completely transformed, to shake off the past. They suffered so much in their families, in their memories, that all they want is to forget; they desire to be born again in almost a literal sense! Some people do this by means of a geographical move, even from one country to another. When this geographical mobility is frequent, it is known in psychology as 'the Marco Polo syndrome'. Others try changing their name. Others change jobs frequently. All of this reflects an intense desire to forget the past and start again, to become a different person. Such people are so anxious to achieve this total change that they attribute to the Holy Spirit a role that was never his intention to play.

Without any doubt, the apostle Paul was right when he said, 'Therefore, if anyone is in Christ, he is a new creation: the old has gone, the new has come!' (2 Cor. 5:17). But we cannot interpret this verse arbitrarily. Does it mean that those who have blue eyes will get brown eyes on conversion? Does it mean that our tempera-ments will be changed and all our memories forgotten? No. If we approach the work of the Holy Spirit in this way, we will be very disappointed and frustrated. Christ gives us new life in the sense that he puts a new nature within us – we are born 'of the Spirit' (Jn. 3:5–6). This produces radical changes: different attitudes, a different perspective on life, a new dignity, a solid sense of per-sonal identity, a new hope for the future, and so we could continue with our list of 'new things'. But God does not promise us the elimination of our painful past or of our limitations here on earth. It is very naïve to expect the Holy Spirit to be a 100% effective psychiatrist. He does not produce a total change in our personalities.

There will indeed come a day when all our 'handicaps and thorns' will disappear, but that will not be until 'the day of Christ Jesus' (Phil. 1:6). Meanwhile, we have to live in a state of tension. Faith is constant tension between two states: we are not the same as we were before, but neither are we yet what God intends us to be or what we ourselves long to become. This tension between the past and the future, that we experience in the present, is a hallmark of Christian faith and will be with us throughout the whole of our lives. The aim of our Christian life is not to get rid of all the tension, or to eliminate all the thorns and handicaps, to feel better and better every day. We grow more and more every day but that does not eliminate the constant tension between what we will be in the future and what we are in the present. We cannot wipe away the past with its traumas and sad memories, but we do have the promise that God will use us not only in spite of our past but through it. This is demonstrated to us in the lives of the patriarchs and of many other heroes of faith.

In this sense, the life of Joseph in the book of Genesis is an extraordinary example of coming to terms and accepting a difficult past. He had a lot of 'heavy baggage' in his biography: born into a family full of conflict, he lost his mother at the age of seven, was spoiled by his father's upbringing, hated by his brothers, and had to face many difficult periods in Egypt. However, when he reviewed all these past events, he had an amazing sense of God's providence. God was not only leading his steps, but using every circumstance in his life in order to accomplish good purposes. His words in Genesis 50:20 are very memorable: 'You intended to harm me, but God meant it for good' (see also 45:5–8). If your life has been difficult so far, you should underline these words in red.

Our past should not cripple us. Some people invest most of their spiritual and psychological energy in trying to heal past memories. I have to confess, as a professional psychiatrist, that very often this is a waste of time. It is better to stop struggling against your past and accept that God uses you, together with your past, however painful or difficult it was. When you are in Christ, you should not view your past as an enemy any more, but as an ally. An ally is someone with whom you work, regardless of whether you like them or not, in order to achieve certain purposes. God does not demand that we like our painful pasts, but he does encourage us to work in alliance with it. This is the essence of accepting your past and being contented with it. Therefore, if we really believe in a God who provides, who is Lord of our lives, the weight of our past takes on a new dimension. If God is for us, what or who can be against us?

The apostle Paul himself had many reasons to regret his past persecution of the new-born church; yet he states with great emphasis in Philippians 3:13, 'But one thing I do: forgetting what is behind and straining towards what is ahead...' Undoubtedly he had experienced that 'in all things God works for the good of those who love him' (Rom. 8:28). Therefore instead of struggling against our pasts, let us trust that God will use them for good. There is a tendency in some circles, both psychological and Christian, to invest too much energy in cleaning the past – but your past was already cleansed when your sins were forgiven.

What is the origin of this state of tension that characterises the life of faith? We cannot be oblivious of the reality that is concealed behind all these obstacles: sin. We are not now referring to specific acts that are contrary to the Word of God – sins – but rather to sin, in the singular, as a state or condition. The ultimate reason for our limitations in prayer, as in every other area of our Christian lives, is to be found in the condition of the human being since the fall. 'I do not understand what I do. For what I want to do I do not do ... I have the desire to do what is good, but I cannot carry it out ... When I want to do good, evil is right there with me' (Rom. 7:15,18,21). The final and total liberation from these bonds will take place when, in our new transfigured bodies, there is no longer any trace of the past state, of sin.

Now we are ready to consider how our entire psychological structure, both temperament and the other dimensions of personality, influences our prayer lives. In this chapter we shall concentrate on two aspects: first, problems related to the dynamics or course of prayer, how to proceed in the act of praying, and then the content of prayer; what we pray. To do so, I have mainly used the specific experiences of believers as a basis for my reflections. For the elaboration of these examples, my guiding criterion has been very straightforward: the frequency of occurrence in everyday experience. It is not intended to be exhaustive; there will undoubtedly be other problems that the reader will not find here, but these are the most frequent.

Problem in the course of prayer

My problem is getting started

> 'I never feel like praying, I'm never in the mood.' 'I would like to pray but I can't.' 'I feel a tremendous lethargy, like a feeling of resistance, almost of rebellion. When I think I have to pray, it seems like a mountainous task and I keep putting it off. I can find time for everything: reading the paper, watching TV, and even reading the Bible or doing Bible study, but praying is always an uphill struggle.'

In a broad sense, this problem is common to all believers. There is in us an element of conflict due to the tension between our spiritual and sinful natures. Prayer is one of the main battlefields where the war described in Romans chapter 7 is fought: 'For what I do is not the good I want to do; no, the evil I do not want to do – this I keep on doing' (v. 19). The devil knows that prayer is one of the believer's key strategies, his 'vital breath'. We should not be surprised by his persistent efforts to ruin this activity. C.S. Lewis, in *The Screwtape Letters*,[1] has magnificently described this striving on the part of the devil to undermine the Christian's prayer life. 'The best thing, where it is possible, is to keep the patient from the serious intention of praying together … to persuade him to something entirely spontaneous, inward, informal and unregularized.' 'Whenever there is prayer, there is danger of his (God's) immediate action.' This accounts for the fact that many of us feel as if a mysterious force is dragging us away from prayer. We should not forget the realities outlined in Ephesians 6:12 – our struggle has to do with spiritual powers, invisible but real. There is a theological reason behind this struggle as we will consider at the end of the chapter.

On a more psychological level, I have already mentioned the temperamental difficulties of extrovert types in general, and of the thinking and sensation types in particular. For these people, settling down to prayer requires a complete change of atmosphere. They have to achieve a state of mind which does not come naturally to them – inward withdrawal, intimacy, the expression of feelings. All this means that these people need adequate external stimuli before embarking on formal prayer.

We find that this problem is aggravated in two situations:

- **perfectionist personalities**. The perfectionist has a natural tendency to put things off. They want to do things so well that they find it very hard to get started. It is only when they have no choice but to start that they find the necessary psychological tension to commence the task. The demands that they make upon themselves are so great that they never seem to find the right circumstances to begin praying, but keep waiting and waiting to be in the right mood to have an excellent prayer time.

- **depressive personalities**. For people of this type, any kind of beginning is excruciating. Depressive people have great difficulties in starting anything. From the moment they get up until they go to bed, their life is a constant battle against all beginnings. They are like cars with cold engines! However, once they manage to start, they can keep going for a long time, enthusiastically engaged in their activities. This is equally true when they pray.

Sometimes their difficulty in starting has deeper roots. Apart from this kind of procrastination described above, some people have a profound resistance for which no logical explanation can be found. These Christians, who are otherwise spiritually alive, want to pray, have a strong desire to do so, but feel unable. The word deep gives us a clue toward an understanding of this phenomenon, which is deeply rooted in their personal biography. It is an unconscious reaction against duty, against whatever they judge to be an obligation. There is a mysterious force hindering them from doing what they should do. A careful examination of their childhood would reveal a strict upbringing, with constant obligations and high expectations on the part of their parents. Later, in adult life, the opposite effect occurs, which in psychology is known as the compensation mechanism. They need to feel free, with no obligations weighing upon them, the exact opposite of what they experienced as children. This is what Paul Tournier termed 'the vengeance of nature'. What we observe is a real allergic reaction to any kind of obligation. The very thought that 'I have to … I must do something,' triggers a negative reaction in them. One way to mitigate this problem might be to help this person see prayer as a pleasure and not so much as a duty.

Occasionally, the matter is further complicated if there have been psychological problems in connection with the father. Rebellion, whether conscious or unconscious, against one's father can be a source of difficulties in our prayer life. This is because we can never entirely separate the concept of the Heavenly Father from that of the earthly father. As a believer matures in the knowledge of God, these problems diminish, but at the beginning of our Christian life, we can find numerous 'points of contact' between the figures of our father and that of God. If our relationship with our parents was one of rebellion or pain, we are likely to transfer some of these negative feelings to God. It is advisable to clarify these concepts with the help of a competent counsellor. Resentment against one's own father can seriously affect the relationship with God; for this reason we must root out any trace of ill-feeling or hatred towards our parents, because otherwise this can block our spiritual growth and our prayer life. This is where the gospel has such an enormous therapeutic value; it is the balm that can heal the deepest wounds. You cannot be a Christian and continue hating your parents: if you are a Christian you have been forgiven, if you have been forgiven, you have to forgive. Forgiveness, peace-making and reconciliation are not only theoretical lessons of our Christian doctrine, but necessary ingredients of our behaviour as disciples.

Incidentally, it should be pointed out that this is the origin of some cases of atheism. The more visceral and aggressive a person's atheistic views are, the more likely they are to have psychological roots, reaching deeply into the person's intimate background. Of course, these emotional conditioning factors do not free such people of their responsibility for disbelieving in God, but they do help us to understand the problem and, consequently, to find an entrance point for effective personal evangelism.

What practical suggestions can we give to a believer who finds it difficult to start praying? First of all, never wait for the right mood. If you do, weeks or months can pass by without a word of prayer. As we will consider in the next chapter, excellency in prayer does not depend on us, but on Christ's merits. To improve your prayer life, do not set high goals: be simple and start small. It is better to pray for five minutes every day than for one hour every three months. Second, try to find the right stimuli to begin. Let us consider some examples. For the depressive person, the presence at his side of a fellow Christian will be very useful. Their character's main enemy is loneliness, especially if they are extroverts. 'If someone is with me, I can pray much more easily. In church, in camps, my prayer life improves a lot' one commented. Of course, this will not always be either possible or desirable, but often the company of another Christian can be a great help to begin to pray.

On other occasions, evangelical hymns will be a stimulus, whether they take the form of a CD or cassette, or simply a hymnbook. The words of many hymns and songs are a source of inspiration, and in fact, singing is itself a form of prayer. Let's not forget that this was exactly the original purpose of many Psalms: prayers to be sung by the Jewish people. At times we can also find help in the prayers of other people – prayers written by great servants of God. The devotional diaries of people like Luther, Wesley, Bunyan, Tozer and many others contain prayers which we can make our own, and from which we can obtain the inspiration to enter the presence of God. Obviously, we must not neglect the most important aid of all: meditation upon the word of God, as we will see in chapter 5.

Try writing down your prayers. One practical exercise I often recommend is to write down two good things that happened today: perhaps some good news, a conversation or any form of blessing for which you feel happy and grateful. Then do the same with two reasons for concern or anxiety. Now you are ready for a short prayer. First, give thanks to God and rejoice about the good from today; then give him your concerns about the negative, sharing all the anxiety that this may have caused you. This exercise may take from five minutes to an hour – you can make it last as long as you wish. You cannot imagine how much it can stimulate you to begin praying. And if you do it regularly, you will discover that in one year you will have praised God for hundreds of blessings and you have developed the discipline of 'Casting all your anxiety upon him' (l Pet. 5:7), which is very therapeutic.

Let us remember that beginning to pray is the most difficult step of all. The battle fought here will be decisive for many victories as well as for defeats.

I don't feel God near me

It seems as if I'm praying to myself.' 'It's as if I were talking to the wall.' 'God seems far away from me.

This absence of feeling is probably the most frequently heard complaint and we have all experienced it at one time or another. It's a sense of unreality, as if I was talking to myself. Even the Psalmists had experiences like this. When we study the Psalms, we are surprised to see how often the word 'far' appears with reference to God. 'Why, O Lord, do you stand far off? Why do you hide yourself in times of trouble?' (Ps. 10:1). 'How long, O Lord? Will you forget me forever? How long will you hide your face from me?' David asks in Psalm 13.

On these occasions when God seems far away the problem is not of course with him. His nearness to us does not depend upon whether we feel him or not. The simple illustration of the sun and the clouds is very useful for understanding this truth. Does the sun shine on cloudy days? The answer is yes. The sun shines, but it does so above the clouds. A cloud may have got in the way and prevented me from seeing and feeling the sun, but the distance between the sun and me has not changed in the slightest. The subjective reality, the reality as I perceive it, is that the sun has stopped shining. The objective reality, however, is that it continues to shine exactly as before. If we could move up above the clouds, our subjective vision would be entirely different.

What are these clouds? What is it that causes our difficulty in feeling? Some of the causes may be momentary: they last for a matter of hours or days and then disappear. These factors will include tiredness and stress. Both of these act upon our capacity to feel in general, not only at a spiritual level. For example, intense stress significantly diminishes one's sexual desire, and the capacity to experience pleasure. Exhaustion, whether physical or emotional, will dry up our feelings. While the state lasts, we are also bound to experience difficulty in feeling God. The more tired we are, the less we are able to feel anything. So if you want to pray and you don't feel God near, the first question you should ask is not, 'Have I sinned? Has God forgotten me?' but, 'Am I fresh – or tired?' One of the symptoms that goes together with tiredness is irritability: you can get angry very easily when you are tired. Most quarrels in families are in the evening, not at breakfast – so be on your guard in the evening!

Stress also affects our spiritual lives a lot especially if it is associated with depression. It distorts the way we see reality. Take two examples from the Bible: Moses, in Numbers chapter 11, is severely depressed. He has suicidal ideas – 'Lord, kill me' (Num. 11:17). This depression was due to exhaustion: 'I am not able to carry this people alone, the burden is too heavy for me' (Num. 11:14). Notice there is no word of rebuke from God: instead, he gives Moses a way out: 'Gather for me seventy men... and they shall bear the burden with you, that you may not bear it alone' (vv. 16–17). Depression is not, in itself, a sin. Because he was stressed and depressed, Moses could not see reality as it was, but saw things in a far darker light. Likewise in the New Testament, when the disciples were rowing on the Sea of Galilee, and a severe storm blew up that threatened their lives, they suffered from stress. Jesus saw them straining at the oars because the wind was against them (Mk. 6:48). When Jesus appears to them, walking on the water, initially they thought he was a ghost – severe stress had distorted their perception (see Matthew 14:2 –33). Often in our prayer lives we will not be able to perceive God because of stress or tiredness.

Like tiredness, depression inhibits our ability to feel. this symptom is called anhedonia: the partial or total inability to feel enjoyment or pleasure. Here there is not only a difficulty in feeling God near – all the feelings have been anaesthetized – but also in being able to begin to pray. The person is uninterested and feels apathetic. This leads the depressed Christian to confuse the cause of the problem – depression – with its consequences – spiritual dryness. It is important to distinguish between these two things in order not to fall prey to feelings of guilt.

This is the personal testimony of one young girl who experienced depression:

> Whenever I raised my voice to God, I felt my own words hitting the ceiling, bouncing off it and crushing me ... 'Who are you talking to? Don't you know that you're being a hypocrite? Don't you realise that you don't feel a word of what you're saying? You're a phoney!' My voice never reached him. There was a pane of glass separating me from God; I knew that he was real, and that he was there, but I just could not feel him; I felt dead. God was a distant being, impossible to reach. I was losing my faith, and at the same time I felt rebellious against God.

Sometimes depression does not have an episodic, fleeting character. Some people have what is known as a *depressive personality* which has similar symptoms to depression but in low intensity and which lasts for years. This is a form of depression that stems from childhood, and is usually the result of traumas suffered in the home environment. A child who is not valued as they should be, who is not encouraged to develop a healthy self-image, will subsequently – as an adult – be dominated by feelings of inadequacy and inferiority. These form the nucleus of a depressive personality. Let's take the example of the young child whose parent thought that the best way of stimulating their emotional growth was by insulting them: 'You're a disaster!' 'You're a good-for-nothing.' 'You'll always be useless.' 'You'll never get anywhere.' Such comments produce in the child the feelings of inadequacy that are typical of chronic depression.

Another characteristic of a depressive is their difficulty in feeling the warmth and love of other people. As they have never learned to experience the love of their first love, their father or mother, they will find it enormously difficult to feel the affection of subsequent loves – a boyfriend, a girlfriend, friends in general and even God himself. Consequently, this person will have relationship problems, not so much because they are unsociable but because they have never felt loved – and the same will happen in their spiritual lives: God will always seem far away. The diagnostic key which reveals that this problem is emotional and not spiritual has to do with the magnitude of the problem. The depressive person has relational problems at every level, not only in their spiritual life. If the problem were only in their relationship with God, due to sin, for instance, their lack of feeling would only affect this sphere. But it is difficult for the depressive person to feel in any intimate relationship.

Sometimes this inability to feel is total. This symptom is known as *affective levelling*, and it can be found in advanced stages of a mental illness, chronic schizophrenia. It is important, then, that the *chronic schizophrenic* should understand, in so far as it is possible, that the origin of their problem is not spiritual, but due to sickness.

So we can see that feelings are very fragile and liable to frequent fluctuations. They are like a fire that goes out and catches again according to the weather conditions; wind fans it up but just a little rain is enough to put it out. Feelings are therefore not a reliable thermometer by which to measure the quality of our prayers – and much less the depth of our faith.

Before we leave this point there is one further question that should be answered: to what extent are feelings really important in prayer? I shall answer this at greater length in subsequent chapters. In anticipation, however, there are three things that need to be considered.

First of all, prayer is an exercise that involves the whole of the human personality. The personality has three dimensions: the will (which is reflected in decisions); the mind (which is expressed in thoughts); and the heart or the emotions (which are expressed in terms of feelings). When praying, these three parts should be kept in harmonious balance, because none of them is superior to any of the others. Prayer ought to have feelings; it cannot be a cold, intellectual exercise. Neither can it be mere emotion, because that would also upset the balance that God requires of us in prayer and in our lives as a whole. The same is true of the mind and the will. In balanced prayer, the whole personality is in action, and not only part of it.

On the other hand, prayer is not something that occurs inside us. It occurs neither inside nor outside us. It occurs 'between'. Prayer is a relationship between God and us. This should free us from the need to centre our preoccupation on our inner state – 'What do I feel? How am I?' Our attention must be fixed on God. So is being introspective good or bad? It depends on how much we do it. Some introspection can bring discernment into our lives. Too much introspection can make us neurotic and leads to self pity. When we cease to look at the Lord and turn our attention inward, we are vulnerable to a subtle temptation from Satan: spiritual hypo-chondria. C.S. Lewis wrote: 'The simplest advice is to turn their gaze away from him towards themselves. Keep them watching their own minds and trying to produce feelings there by the action of their wills.'[2]

Lastly, we need to learn to distinguish between feeling God and an awareness of God. These are different realities. To feel God all the time is an act of exclusion. By definition, while I am feeling God I cannot do or think anything else. It requires my total attention: otherwise, the feeling disappears. By contrast, developing an awareness of God in my life is to become conscious of the continuous presence of the Lord in me. In other words, it is to be conscious of God. This is not exclusive, because it constitutes a vital attitude, it is a way of living. I can be immersed in an activity that fully absorbs me and, therefore, be incapable of feeling God. But I know, I am aware, that God is there, that he is within me. Nicholas Herman of Lorraine, better known as Brother Lawrence, put this into practice in a most admirable way. In the midst of his duties as cook, he practised what he called 'a habitual, silent, secret conversation with God'. And his advice was that 'we should develop an awareness of God's presence by conversing continuously with him'.[3]

This beautiful spiritual reality is what the Bible describes as 'the fear of the Lord'. God is so central to our lives that he presides over everything. This is walking with God as Enoch did (Gen. 5:24). This is living as seeing 'him who is invisible' (Heb. 11:27). This is seeking the presence of the Lord in our daily walk: 'If your presence does not go with us…' (Ex. 33:15).

So then, we do not so much need to feel God as to develop an awareness of God in our daily lives.

I don't want to be hypocritical when I pray

I can only come to God if I'm really sincere. I don't want to pray out of obligation, because it's the time to pray, out of routine. I want my prayers to always have a special dimension of authenticity.

This woman, speaking from her heart, reflects another problem. She wants her prayers to be spontaneous and sincere. For this reason, she waits until she is in the best possible spiritual 'shape' because, otherwise, she feels as if she is pretending: she only prays, then, when she really feels like doing so.

Let us consider the testimony of another young girl:

> In order to come into the presence of God, I used to have to feel accepted by myself, and clean. As this was hardly ever the case, I either didn't pray, or my prayer became a struggle. Not because God didn't accept me, but because I did not accept myself.

People like this are usually insecure and perfectionist, with a generous dose of idealism and a marked emphasis on feelings. Lacking self-acceptance, they put great emphasis on being sincere. They understand prayer to be an emotional relationship to which they can have access when they feel right. It goes without saying that the devil will exploit this type of personality to keep the person from praying altogether. Hence the need for a certain amount of discipline. Sometimes it is necessary to pray even though, in terms of form, it just seems like an empty ritual. The Lord abhors ritual when it comes from hearts that are far from him (Is. 1:10ff). It is not ritual in itself that God rejects, but the cold hearts and the lack of love beyond the rituals. So method is not a bad thing in itself. As we have seen, prayer is a concentration not only of feelings, but also of the will.

My recommendation, then, is basically the same one that I suggested for those who have problems starting to pray: begin praying, regardless of what you feel. It is better to begin praying, though one doesn't feel like it, than not to pray at all. Prayer is not primarily an expression of my inner well-being, but of my love towards God. I do not pray when I feel well; I pray because I love the Lord.

I find it impossible to concentrate

> I start to pray but I cannot concentrate my attention for
> longer than a minute. My mind wanders around a thou-
> sand-and-one concerns. Suddenly I realise that my thoughts
> are not on what I am doing, but far away on the business of
> that day.

This is another frequent problem – a lack of concentration, the wandering mind. We have already seen how
this affects the sensation type, because of the multitude
of impressions and stimuli that crowd into their minds.
Besides the temperamental factor, we find two other situations in which this difficulty arises:

a) An anxious or nervous character
These are people whose minds are full of anxious
thoughts and deep concerns. There is always some
cloud or other on their horizon; they worry dispropor-
tionately about everything. At the same time they are
usually hypersensitive, which makes them anticipate
events going wrong. They are always imagining bad
news, and can do nothing except concentrate on their
problems and they cannot relax. Concentration on anything else is difficult due to their high level of inner
tension. They are always on the alert, always restless,
and sit perched on the edge of their chairs. As a hymn
puts it, 'the mind wanders quickly and uncertainly'.
When one problem has been resolved, they are already
thinking about the next one. They live without a
moment's peace or rest, and concentrating on prayer is
difficult. What's more, they have a propensity to be
obsessive – they dwell on the same thing for hours and
can't get it out of their minds, no matter how hard they
try. These believers suffer when they pray because their

lack of concentration breaks the thread of their prayer time.

Allied to this kind of personality, we find another equally hostile enemy of concentration: haste. Due to their restlessness, they live and do everything in a hurry. Their life is a continuous maelstrom. In view of the inherent characteristics of prayer, it is not hard to see why this haste is a serious obstacle. Jung's dictum is on target with regard to this problem: 'Haste is not of the devil: it is the devil.' It is very difficult to find the right spirit for recollection and meditation if we are harassed by haste.

b) Bad thoughts during prayer

> While I'm praying, blasphemous thoughts come to my mind, insults and images that are offensive to the Lord. I don't want to have such thoughts, but they force their way into my mind as if there were another person inside me. It's like a parasite that I can't shake off.

Surprisingly, this was the experience of a spiritual giant: Spurgeon. He writes in his autobiography, 'I remember times, in my earliest Christian days, when there came into my mind thoughts so evil that I clapped my hand to my mouth for fear I should be led to give utterance to them. This is one way in which Satan tortures those whom God has delivered out of his hand. Many of the choicest saints have been thus molested.'

This painful problem often arises in obsessive personalities. An obsession is a persistent and absurd image or idea, an unwanted thought that clings to the mind, in conflict with our will. Those who suffer from these obsessions don't agree with such thoughts: indeed, they strongly dislike them. Sometimes obsessive ideas are related simply to their mood, or to anxiety, in which case they are of a fleeting nature. But when they are persistent, we are in the presence of real, obsessive neurosis, which requires professional treatment. In such situations it is important to remember that this problem has no spiritual cause. It is very disturbing to these Christians to imagine that such bad thoughts come from sin or from any spiritual deficiency. This is why we need to clarify their confusion. Unwanted bad thoughts during prayer are the symptom of an emotional disturbance which requires psychological help. Usually sufferers experience great relief through this simple illustration: 'If you were to write down on a piece of paper the ideas and images that harass you as you pray, would you sign your name to it?' The answer is always categorically negative. This helps the person see that these ideas are alien to their consciousness, and have nothing to do with their desires, their will or their spirituality – and that the problem does not arise from sin. The consequences, however, may eventually affect their spiritual life because these ideas have a discouraging effect on the believer. As Spurgeon suggested, the devil can take advantage of our weak points and torment us with this strategy, giving rise to doubts and confusion in the believer. But remember: the cause of this is not primarily a spiritual one.

There are many practical recommendations for increasing our concentration while we pray. One of the best ways is praying not just mentally, but verbally – to articulate thoughts in words. We can do this either quietly or out loud. Remember how Hannah, the mother of Samuel, asked earnestly for a child: 'As she continued praying before the Lord, Eli observed her mouth. Hannah was speaking in her heart, only her lips moved...' (1 Sam. 1:12–13). Others have found that writing down their prayers has been very helpful. It is also important to set aside the time of day when there is least tension, perhaps the late evening, when the day's activities are over. A timetable like this will help anyone who is prone to anxiety because mornings – when many concerns crowd into their minds – tend to be the worst time for them. In any case, there are no fixed rules. Everything that helps to enhance concentration is to be welcomed.

Some people like to use mental images, for example, centring attention on the persons of the Trinity. The most accessible mental image of all is that of Jesus. This method has its ardent supporters and also its opponents. It is our view that the risk of idolatry is not present when the images we use are exclusively mental images. Imagining a scene from the life of Jesus, and fixing our attention on it can be useful in some cases. We must stress, however, that each person must use whatever they find to be most beneficial.

I can't pray in public

Some believers have no problem praying alone or in very small groups, but any public contribution, such as in a prayer meeting in their church, is an impossibility for them. This is generally the problem of shy people, especially when their shyness has to do with feelings of anxiety. In such cases, it is my suggestion that their prayers should be brief, just a sentence or two, with the attention always centred on God and never on the people present. Beginning with these short, concise prayers, they will find public prayer easier. However, if the difficulty is intense, I recommend a deeper analysis of the underlying psychological problem: the right kind of psychotherapy or counselling might be beneficial here.

In any case, a believer should never be forced to pray in public. Some people are tormented by the thought of having to pray in front of others. We must respect their emotional difficulty. The psychological hindrances that some people experience have nothing to do with their degree of commitment or maturity. The greater the pressure on a person, the more difficult it will be for them to pray. This is due to the aura of expectation that envelops them at that moment and which falls on them like a slab of concrete, leaving them completely paralysed.

So far we have seen some problems in prayer, basic-ally related to our emotional makeup. Before we close this section, we should emphasize what we have already anticipated. Ultimately we have to understand all these difficulties in the context of a spiritual warfare. They are not just psychological problems but existential – spirit-ual ones. As Christians, we are caught up in a battle that takes place both at a cosmic and at a personal level. 'For our struggle is not against flesh and blood, but against the rulers, against the authorities, against the powers of this dark world and against the spiritual forces of evil in the heavenly realms' (Eph. 6:12). Our life is a battlefield between two opposite forces, the flesh and the spirit (1 Pet. 2:11). One of the main weapons in this warfare is prayer: 'Pray in the Spirit on all occasions with all kinds of prayers and requests. With this in mind, be alert and always keep on praying for all the saints' (Eph. 6:18). This is why we need the discipline of a soldier and the efforts of an athlete to 'fight the good fight of the faith' and 'to finish the race' (1 Tim. 6:12; 2 Tim. 4:7). So, in one sense, prayer is a pleasure to enjoy, but in another sense, it is a discipline to be practised because it belongs to the essential armour of the Christian soldier.

Are we then to draw from all this a negative conclusion about prayer? Is prayer nothing but a succession of problems? By no means: prayer is the vehicle of great blessing, in spite of all these problems. And in the midst of all these difficulties, let us never forget that 'the Spirit helps us in our weakness ... intercedes for us with groans that words cannot express' (Rom. 8:26). The day will come when the glorious promise of God will be fulfilled: 'Behold, I am making everything new' (Rev. 21:5). From that day on, all the obstacles which now limit our relationship with Christ and make us 'see through a glass, darkly' (1 Cor. 13:12 KJV), will vanish, and we shall see 'face to face'. The state that presently strait-jackets our prayer – sin – will have disappeared completely, and, free from all limitation, 'God himself' (Rev. 21:3b) will dwell with us.

Problems in the content of prayer – the balanced prayer

So far I have presented the difficulties which arise in the course of prayer, either at the beginning, in its development or at the end. This is what we call the dynamics of prayer. Now we still have to consider the problems of prayer in its contents, it is important to consider not just *how* we pray, but also *what* we pray for. There is an old Spanish proverb, 'Tell me who you walk with and I will tell you who you are.' The same could be said of prayer; 'Tell me what you pray for and I will tell you what kind of Christian you are.' What we pray for gives an excellent insight into our spirituality.

The believer who looks for a balanced life of prayer will try to include the four essential aspects that the Bible, especially the New Testament, teaches us. But we must take care to avoid errors. An undue emphasis on any of those aspects, when it happens constantly, causes unbalanced prayers and can be symptomatic of deeper problems, either with our Christian lives or with our emotional structures. In prayer, something can happen that is similar to our diet. The healthiest diet is the one which contains the adequate balance of carbohydrates, proteins, fats, fibre, etc. If somebody is fed exclusively with proteins, they can have problems. In the same way, when a believer systematically uses only one of the constituent elements of prayer we are facing a warning signal.

Let us examine the ingredients of a balanced prayer and also the emotional problems which can be hidden behind their respective imbalances. This will help us to summarize the concepts of temperament and personality that we have already considered. The ingredients of our prayer reflect the threefold dimension of our relationships: with God, with ourselves and with other people. Before the fall, these three basic relationships were kept in perfect harmonious balance. A harmonious life in these relationships will have its manifestation in balanced prayers, and so the imbalances in our prayer lives give us clues to certain problems in these relationships.

Adoration and praise: focusing attention on God himself

This is speaking to God about himself and is connected to the first basic relationship: our relationship with him. It is the way in which many Psalms begin and the prayers of many believers start in the same way: concentrating our attention on God's attributes: his power, his faithfulness, his greatness. We meditate on what God is and does. This takes us spontaneously to an attitude which should be present throughout the whole course of prayer: gratitude. Praise should be the first part of our prayers, and if it isn't, it could be that our prayer life is too selfish and self-centred. Sometimes we start our prayers by focusing on our own needs, and we should not do this.

Since it is an expression of feeling, praise and adoration will be more difficult to the thinking type. Even when they come to develop certain feelings, they find it hard to show them and even harder to put them into words. Adoration will be something they have to learn and develop. On the contrary, this aspect of prayer will be simple and spontaneous to the sensation type. Their automatic prayer at the sight of a sunset is full of adoration to God the Creator: but this adoration will be more difficult in the silent solitude of their quiet time. They need an outside stimulus to move them to worship. In the case of the feeling type, praise will spring up as a result of inner inducements: the hearing of music or a noble deed, perhaps. This stimulates them much more than anything which comes through the senses, as it works through the feelings. They do not experience many difficulties in worshipping during private devotions: relationships come easily to them. No doubt it is the intuitive type, gifted with an easy spirituality, who will give most time to adoration. A rich imagination makes it possible for them to contemplate the greatness of God in a vivid way.

When adoration and praise are the only ingredient of our prayers we must review our concept of spirituality. It is possible to fall into a superficial mysticism which can conceal the need to escape from ourselves or – more frequently – from the world around us. We can be trying to escape from realities which are too hard to accept. In our relationship with God we cannot put aside our horizontal relationships. I shall go deeper into this point in chapter 5. An unbalanced spirituality can lead to some of the mistakes of medieval monasticism. Even if we do not shut ourselves away in a monastery in the literal sense, we can live in a similar way by forgetting our duties in the other areas of relationships – to ourselves (in request and confession) and to others (in intercession). We have to be careful of super-spirituality. Zeal is not the supreme test of spirituality and a spirituality born from a desire to escape from reality is a fleshly spirituality.

Confession: speaking to God about our sins

This point brings us into the second relationship: the relation with ourselves. This dimension of prayer is often a consequence of the preceding one. As we shall consider later, to see ourselves in the mirror (God) makes us aware of our unworthiness. The clearer the mirror is, and the better we know God, the more unworthy we feel. So it is important that we get to know God rightly. God is not a projection of ourselves. It is interesting to see how in many Scripture texts, both dimensions – adoration and confession – are entwined. Our confession must include our sins by commission and also our shortcomings by omission. Not only the evil that we have done, but also the good that we have left undone must be confessed.

According to the psychological types, the thinking type will be the most faithful in this aspect. Weakest in the area of adoration, they are the strongest in this area. No Christian is perfect: we all have strengths and weaknesses in the different areas of spirituality. The thinking type has a concern for uprightness and justice and a capacity for introspection and self-analysis which provide a sense of easiness, compared to the other temperaments, when confessing. It may be most difficult for the sensation type to be conscious of sin; they are poor at introspection, because they are always looking outwards. As soon as they are aware of sin, however, a sincere confession takes place. The apostle Peter is a prototype of the sensation type, and his experience after his denial of the Lord is a good example: 'And Peter remembered the saying of Jesus, "Before the cock crows, you will deny me three times." And he went out and wept bitterly' (Mt. 26:75 RSV).

Where is the unbalance here? An important principle in the matter of guilt is that it is possible to be guilty without feeling it, and to feel guilty without being guilty. The first is what the Bible calls a 'hardened conscience'. But let us centre our thought on the second part of the sentence. A subjective guilt feeling does not always correspond with an objective reality of sin. In this case we have what is called false or morbid guilt. This is not the appropriate place to consider the distinction between real and false guilt; it is enough to admit that there are guilt feelings which have their origin in neurotic problems. Let us take as an example the over-scrupulous, unhealthy conscience of someone who suffers from obsessive neurosis. For example, I knew a young man who spent three hours a day – every day – in confession. The balance was completely broken. His constant doubting, his vague guilty feelings were more due to insecurity – 'I don't know whether I have sinned, I don't know whether I have done the wrong thing' – than to a concrete misdeed.

However, I must emphasize what I said before about these obsessive problems: unless the underlying psycho-

logical cause is solved, they can have spiritual consequences, such as a crisis of faith. In the case mentioned
above, the young man concentrated all his prayer in confession. He spent the whole day confessing to God. But
as he did not feel pardoned – logically he could not feel
pardoned because he had not sinned – he began to have
doubts about God. He went through a period of spiritual cooling until he understood the true nature of the
problem.

This unhealthy conscience, which is constantly accus-
ing and begets many false guilt feelings, is also manifested in people with inferiority complexes or a poor self
image. Likewise, we can find unbalance in confession
during a period of depression. Some forms of depression
are distinguished by deep guilt feelings: in fact, false
guilt is one of the key symptoms of depression. During
the depressive episode the believer can feel constantly
accused. One of the most striking examples in the history of Christianity is that of John Bunyan. He was a
great saint, but was also very tormented by deep emotional disturbances. The author of *The Pilgrim's Progress*
went through such periods of torturing guilt feelings
that often his Christian life became a source of pain
rather than of joy. In *Grace Abounding to the Chief of
Sinners*, Bunyan has left us his spiritual autobiography
which is an excellent example of these morbid guilt feelings and depressive, obsessional thoughts. Sometimes
these feelings compelled him to flee from God.

After surmounting a long depression, a Christian
said: 'I ran away from prayer because I felt accused by
God.' These problems may affect our spiritual life
because we are a unity. For this reason we need to
understand the whole picture and treat the whole person: otherwise we might create more confusion in the
tormented Christians. We should also remember that

God uses neurotic people – vessels of clay. He uses broken people who come from broken homes. He can use you and me, in all and through all our emotional disorders.

Before we close this section on guilt and confession, we need to get to the core of the Christian faith: the cross of Christ. Guilt is not primarily related to our self-image but to God's holiness. As Christians we feel guilty not because we failed to achieve our goals, but because we offended the Father first and hurt our neighbour second. It may certainly have hurt me, but it hurts God much more. The words of the Prodigal Son are a brilliant summary of this principle: 'Father, I have sinned against heaven and against you. I am no longer worthy to be called your son' (Lk. 15:21). Therefore, confession is not just a psychological expression of personal frustration, but the conviction that we have offended God. Notice David's words after his sin: 'Against you, you only, have I sinned and done what is evil in your sight' (Ps. 51:4). Once we get this deep conviction, we turn to the cross where the soothing grace of Christ relieves any feelings of true guilt through forgiveness: 'Come now, let us reason together, says the Lord. Though your sins are like scarlet, they shall be as white snow; though they are red like crimson, they shall become like wool' (Is. 1:18). Christ's forgiveness on the cross is the supreme expression of the therapeutic value of the gospel. Then our prayers of confession are a gift and a blessing from God.

Request: speaking to God about our needs

This area of prayer is concerned with the second vital relationship – with ourselves. It is also the aspect of prayer which requires the smallest effort, as we all are always ready to request! It is an integral and legitimate part of prayer, and the Lord Jesus Christ himself exhorted his disciples to use it. We do not have to feel selfish and guilty when we ask for something. It will be good, however, if we remember the biblical condition: our request must be according to the will of God, and in the name of Jesus (Jn. 14:13–14). We cannot ask according to our fancies, seeking mainly pleasure (Jas. 4:3). We shall succeed in our petitionary prayers as long as we live in fellowship with the Lord himself (Jn. 15:7), abiding in him. We cannot expect God to treat as a father would if we do not behave like his children.

The clearest unbalance here is to make of prayer an egocentric exercise of constant requests. A young man said to me: 'Sometimes I have the impression that I approach God in a manner comparable to the way I go to a supermarket, with a long list of needs that I present one by one.' We have to struggle constantly against our selfishness in order to avoid this type of prayer, which is completely centred on ourselves and our needs. Requests are pleasing to God because he is a loving father who wants to satisfy us. But when I do not behave like a son, trying to please and love his father, God becomes my servant, I try to manipulate him – perhaps unconsciously – and I reduce prayer to its most primitive form.

Consequently, this part of prayer is not subject so much to temperamental aspects, as to moral components. Our selfishness does not depend on temperament; it comes from the heart: we are all basically selfish. For this reason we do not find significant differences here according to the psychological types. Instead, it seems obvious that emotional maturity does exert an influence. The more immature or primitive the person is, the more they make themselves the centre of their lives. Their world, their needs, their problems are the centre of gravity in their existence. They act as if they should have to spend all their emotional energy on themselves, with nothing being left for others. Some people pray only when they have needs and they do not really understand what God is like. They can see God as an aspirin – someone who will solve all their potential headaches. This behaviour is quite normal in children, to such an extent that its persistence in the adult is a symptom of stagnation in the psychological development, leading to what are described as primitive personalities. The motto of their lives seems to be 'get, get, get', and they are the paradigm of immaturity. Christ's remark is exactly the opposite: 'It is more blessed to give than to receive' (Acts 20:35). That is a sign of emotional, psychological and spiritual maturity.

As we think about requests, we have to concentrate on thanksgiving. This is one of the most beautiful parts of prayer and yet one of the most neglected. How often we forget to say 'Thank you' to God! We are always ready to ask, but when he answers positively, we forget to express our gratitude. This fact shows a reality deeper than a mere lack of politeness. Saying 'Thank you' is not just a matter of courtesy, but an expression of recognition and even love. It is remarkable how this problem was at the very root of our broken relationship with God. We read in Romans 1:21, 'For although they knew God, they neither glorified him as God nor gave thanks to him.' We see here how adoration and gratitude are closely linked. While adoration is an inner attitude, gratitude is the outward expression of this attitude. As Paul explains the different steps that led man to reject God, the lack of gratitude plays an important role. In the same way that many human relationships – such as marriage – suffer a lot when there is no gratitude, our personal relationship with God may be severely affected when we hardly ever say 'Thank you'. Thanksgiving, therefore, is an essential component in our prayers: 'Do not be anxious about anything, but in everything, by prayer and petition, with thanksgiving, make your requests known to God' (Phil. 4:6).

Intercession: speaking to God about other people

This is one of the most noble aspects of prayer: to use its power in order to help others. The Bible contains many examples of intercessory prayer. From Abraham to the apostles we find a long list of tenacious intercessors. But no doubt the climax is found in the person of Jesus. He is the supreme model. For example, his prayer in John chapter 17 is the expression of a strong love, even at a moment of great suffering and intense personal needs. On that very day facing Gethsemane's agonies, Jesus had many reasons to concentrate on his own needs and forget others. Yet what a paradigm of prayer! He forgets himself and displays a magnificent expression of pure love; he is genuinely interested in the well-being and the peace of those near him – the apostles – but also of all 'those who will believe in me through their word' (v. 20). He interceded for others because he loved them. This is the only secret of intercession.

Therefore to pray for others is the result of the *agape* that God puts in our heart; it is the fruit of the Spirit. That is the reason why it must be cultivated. But for many of us, intercession is the Cinderella of our prayers. We hardly devote to it the 'postscript' of our time. We are enthusiastic in praise; we feel overwhelmed in confession; we indulge in a festival of self-centredness in our requests. But to remember other people ... that is quite another story! Therefore, we can never have an excess of intercessory prayer. Its abundance is never negative. We need to foster our love for others through prayer, that the Lord may give us a true pastoral heart, sensitivity with regard to the needs of others, those of our churches, those of our friends. How much time do we spend in intercession in comparison with the time devoted to the other three elements? If we desire a balanced prayer life, we cannot neglect any of its four constituents. The amount of time given to intercession may become a good test of our selfishness.

Of the psychological types, the thinking type will be the most orderly and methodical in their intercessory life, particularly concerned for justice and righteousness. The sensation type, especially the introvert, with their strong sense of responsibility, can be a good organizer of prayer meetings. Here again, if intercession is a difficult area for you, start with very small 'projects': if you only pray for one person a week, that will be 52 people a year, so start small lists and build up to something longer.

One last remark. Let us remember that the different parts of prayer are a reflection of our relationships. We cannot be so busy with others that we forget God or ourselves. Frantic activism, even in the form of service for other people, should not jeopardise our close fellowship with God or an adequate concern for ourselves. Activism is the worst enemy of prayer and the sensation type – particularly the extrovert one, whose prototypes are business-people – should be particularly careful here. Otherwise the outcome will be exhaustion and spiritual drought.

Jeremiah: chiaroscuros in the prayers of a prophet

Thus far we have considered how prayer presents certain difficulties. Sometimes these are related to problems involving our personality or our temperament; at other times they are related to passing circumstances, such as depression, exhaustion, doubts and loneliness. Before closing this chapter, let us centre our attention on the word of God itself. In the book of Jeremiah we find a prayer (Jer. 20:7–18) that is an admirable synthesis of what I have developed up to this point: the combined influence of emotional, spiritual and environmental aspects in a believer's life and its consequence on prayer. Let us look at it in detail.

Regarding his temperament, we see in Jeremiah characteristics that would include him in the introverted group and that define him as a person with a great natural sensitivity. This sensitivity is seen in small but very significant details. For example, his perception of nature (24:1–10) demonstrates something more than just an ordinary knowledge. As R.K. Harrison, the Old Testament scholar, says, 'Jeremiah was a nature lover.'[4] Quite possibly he was predominantly an intuitive and feeling type.

We are told nothing about his biographical development except that he came from a family of priests (1:1). From this we can sense a religious family environment. Contrary to what some commentators think, in my opinion he was not a depressive person. The reason for his frequent crisis of sadness must be explained at a deeper level: in his spiritual sensitivity. In effect, the prophet had reached such a developed degree of maturity with the Lord that he looked at the reality around him with God's eyes. The lamentable situation of the people caused him great pain, almost to the point of making his heart bleed (cf. 15:18). This pain was so strong not because Jeremiah was neurotic but because he had learned to see situations and people from God's point of view. In the same way that Jesus could not stop weeping upon entering Jerusalem (Mt. 23:37–39), Jeremiah too could not hold back his tears upon experiencing so directly the wounds produced by his desperate environment. The tears of a Christian are sometimes a sign of spiritual maturity: blessed are those who mourn.

We also need to consider Jeremiah's circumstances. Originally called against his will (1:6; 20:7), he lived in what was almost total solitude (15:17), without family (16:1–2), without possessions (12:7–8), relentlessly pursued and persecuted (18:18) even by his friends (20:10). Mockery and scorn were his habitual companions (20:7b).

It is not strange, then, that in the midst of this situation he should go through frequent periods of crisis in his relationship with God. He did not understand the Lord's sovereignty: he felt perplexed regarding his plans and purposes (12:1–4). His questions produce much the same response in many people today. 'Why? How is it possible for a just God to allow so much injustice?'

Additionally, all his efforts seemed to be in vain. He had paid a high price without seeing any results (11:7–8). Jeremiah's ministry was apparently sterile. From a human point of view, it was a complete failure (7:23–26).

The interdependency of all these factors, an introverted temperament together with a great capacity to feel, an exquisite spiritual sensitivity and the concrete circumstances of the moment are beautifully expressed in the prayer recorded in chapter 20. With this passage, Scripture has left us a legacy of a living and practical summary on the complexity and simplicity of prayer. This prayer of Jeremiah is a masterpiece of what we could call the *spiritual chiaroscuro*. It is characterized by a blend of light and shadows. These pictorial contrasts are what give it a strength, a beauty and a realism with which every believer can identify. These *chiaroscuros* are a reflection of our own relationship with God.

The tenebrism[5] of this prayer is not surprising. As a whole it forms a lament that is perfectly understandable in the light of the situation described. Jeremiah had a great faith in his all-powerful Lord (32:17,27), but he was a man of flesh and blood. This is why he pours all the heaviness of his heart upon the Lord. The passage begins with several complaints. The prophet protests about the ministry to which God has 'deceived' or seduced him (20:7). Today we would speak about a vocational frustration. He laments the fact that all his work brings no results and the reaction of mockery that he receives as reward (v. 8). He nevertheless recognizes that the Lord has infected him with a mysterious zeal to present his word and now he cannot keep quiet: 'His word is in my heart like a burning fire, shut up in my bones. I am weary of holding it in: indeed, I cannot' (v. 9). He continues to complain, with reason, about the opposition, and even the literal persecution, he has received from those closest to him (v. 10). In fact, he complains about everything.

At this point I have a question: Is it right for a man of God to use prayer as a vehicle of protest? Is this logical in a mature believer? Where is the praise, the adoration, the intercession for others? In his desperation, Jeremiah complains openly. He had already done so on other occasions, even using strong language, with a judgmental tone: 'I bring a case before you' (12:1).[6] And on each of these occasions I do not find words of reprimand from God. Even when the prophet pours out his disgust very vehemently, the Lord does not reprove him. Why does God have an understanding attitude and not one of condemnation in view of this prayer? I believe there are two reasons:

First of all, Jeremiah protested from a position of loyalty and complete submission to God. He could complain against the Lord because he was on the Lord's side; he was doing it from a position of obedience. When this happens, the sincere expression of our anger or of our doubts is not a negation of integrity but a manifestation of it. Integrity and sincerity go together. It is not sin to tell God in prayer how we feel, even though some – or many – of our words may be wrong. God delights more in honesty, even if it be bold, than in a superficial faith that is free from tension and fight. We cannot forget that, psychologically, the greatest obstacle to accepting and forgiving others is repressed anger.

The second reason lies in what we would call 'the two sides' of protest. Many conflict relationships often have a paradox with which we must be familiar. At first sight, because Jeremiah is fighting God, he seems to reject God. Apparently his rebelliousness expresses estrangement. Nevertheless, the reality is almost the contrary: Jeremiah, in his complaint against God, is coming nearer to God. The prophet's struggle is the conflict of a lover. His apparent estrangement and rejection are born out of the intense desire to approach God to find light and strength. If Jeremiah were removed from God, he would not be fighting him: he would merely be indifferent. Tension and conflict are very often an expression of closeness, not of indifference. We also see this in family relationships, both among spouses as well as between parents and children. Deep down in my heart, I can be very close to God when outwardly it seems as though there is rebellion inside me. God does not tolerate arrogance and pride in our prayers. But he does allow negative feelings to be expressed when they come from a lover's heart overcome with sorrow and pain. If prayer becomes defiance, we are going to offend the Lord. On the other hand, when it seeks to encounter God face to face, it leads to a greater intimacy even though this may imply struggle.

Thus far the shadows of the painting. A glimmer of light suddenly appears in the midst of all the darkness. Jeremiah is a man overcome with pain, but not defeated; overwhelmed by suffering but not sunken: in a crisis of faith, but not distant from God. This is why it comes up suddenly, like a shining ray of light, the splendour of a declaration of an unbreakable trust. 'But the Lord is with me like a mighty warrior' (20:11). No doubt this had been the support of his life from the very day of his calling: 'Before I formed you in the womb I knew you, before you were born I set you apart ... Do not be afraid ... for I am with you' (1:5,8).

In spite of the fragility of his feelings, Jeremiah had a fountain of strength: the promise of the intimate and constant presence of God. 'They will fight against you but will not overcome you, for I am with you' (1:19). This secret enabled him to obtain strength from weakness in the midst of so much adversity.

The light period reaches a crescendo, like a symphony, until it bursts forth in an open praise, 'Sing to the Lord! Give praise to the Lord!' (20:13). The contrast between this joy and the shadows of the previous laments could not be greater. It is the same man. It is the same prayer. They are the same circumstances. What has happened? Jeremiah, for the moment, has ceased to look inside himself and he fixes his eyes upon God. The self-vindicating prophet that protested about almost everything (verses 7–10) now passes on to genuine praise. The key to this change lies in the centre of his meditation. If he concentrates on himself, he only sees the disgrace that afflicts him and he falls into self-pity, 'Look, Lord, what's the matter with me? Don't you care about me?' But if he lifts his eyes to his source of help and strength, then the darkness is changed into light. Too much introspection leads to desperation; lifting up our eyes to God leads to renewal and inspiration. If I had been writing the book of Jeremiah, I would have stopped here. I would prefer that kind of Christian life.

Nevertheless, we soon return to the darkness. Another sudden change: 'Cursed be the day I was born! May the day my mother bore me not be blessed' (v. 14). A sudden relapse that this time seems to be more intense. As if he had broken apart emotionally, Jeremiah falls fully into a depression. The vehemence of his curses (vv. 14–15), his wishes for death (v. 17), his fastidiousness and pain in the face of life, are all unequivocal symptoms of a deep depression.

How is it possible to go so fast from spiritual euphoria to the most absolute darkness? That is where the strength of this prayer actually lies and it gives it a classical dimension, in the sense that its value can be applied to all believers in all the ages. In the first part we find a man who, while burdened down and going through a crisis, even so has not lost his trust. Then a man appears renewed with the joy of the Lord, a man who, nevertheless, has not lost his inner pain. The realism of the word of God is extraordinary! There is no place for euphoria. The Christian life, including prayer, is a succession of lighter and darker periods, of lights and shadows, of ups and downs.

Such oscillations do not express emotional instability or mental disturbance. Jeremiah was not an immature person carried about 'by any which wind' that would shake a weak personality or a mediocre commitment to his Lord. Rather, the opposite was true. These contrasts were – are – characteristic of the inner struggle of every believer. A prayer life is a great way of expressing faith, but also of expressing pain. God accepts both.

May God free us from defeatism; not everything is shadow, there are lights. But may he free us as well from super-spiritualism and triumphalism; not everything is light, there are also shadows.

---

1 C.S. Lewis, The Screwtape Letters (London: Geoffrey Bles Edit., 1954), pp24, 26

2 C.S. Lewis, The Screwtape Letters, p23. Note this is the advice of one devil to another to stop spiritual maturity being achieved!

3 N. Herman of Lorraine, The Practice of the Presence of God (London: Allenson & Co. Ltd.)

4 R.K. Harrison, Jeremiah and Lamentatuins, Tyndale Commentaries (UK: Inter-Varsity Press, 1973), p.36

5 Tenebrism (from Ital. tenebroso, murky) is the name given to painting (particularly seventeenth-century Neapolitan and Spanish) in a very low key, that is, having a low tone and colour value; the contrast between the light and shadow areas being accentuated, creating a pictorial play of lights and shadows

6 '. . . I would plead my case with Thee.' NASV

Chapter 3

THE THERAPEUTIC VALUE OF PRAYER

Prayer, a love relationship

Prayer produces certain evident consequences in the believer. It is impossible to decide which of these effects are spiritual and which are emotional, but all of them are therapeutic. As has been explained earlier, man is an indivisible unit formed by body, mind and spirit: as a result, we cannot nor do we wish to separate these effects. They are intimately united as one. It must be affirmed, however, that prayer is not just a source of spiritual blessings. It is also the vehicle of emotional well-being that has brought relief to the tormented mind of many people throughout the centuries. As an observer of human nature and as a Christian professional in psychotherapy, I can testify to the psychotherapeutic effects of prayer. No secular psychologist, who considers him or herself to be impartial and sensible, can deny the unparalleled therapeutic value of faith in general and of prayer in particular. I am referring to biblical faith: not to an enslaving religion that can be more a form of neurosis than of liberation.

Vernon Grounds, an American theologian and sociologist, writes,

Health and mental healing require forgiveness as the antidote against guilt; they require fellowship as the antidote
against alienation; power as the antidote against impotence, and hope as the antidote against desperation. This is
why I continue to ask myself: Where ought we to find the
provision for all these psychological needs? The most
appropriate place is the Gospel, to the point that it is
changed into an unrivalled antidote against neurosis. I
would dare to say that if health and mental healing require
an understanding of the 'I', an identity of the self, an
acceptance of the self, a liberation of the self, if this is its
demand, then the Gospel of Jesus Christ has extraordinary
resources for restoring mental health.[1]

Grounds has not been the only one to demonstrate the
experiential evidence of the value of faith in mental
health. Wayne Oates,[2] among other notable English-
speaking authors, is also worthy of mention. In the
Hispanic field, the book *Más Allá de la Psiquiatría (Beyond
Psychiatry)*[3] by Abraham Genis and Angel Brun presents
the combined perspective of a psychiatrist and of a pastor. There are many professional references that point to
a single reality: the therapeutic implications of a balanced and biblical faith.

But not all religion is good and, in fact, some religions
are clearly damaging to one's mental health. The Lord
Jesus himself denounced all kinds of legalism in his
fiercest diatribes against the Pharisees (Mt. 23:13–36). In
the same way, we must recognise that certain forms of
prayer are so primitive or so unbalanced that they come
to discredit the faith and Christians themselves. Prayer
ought to be the result of an inner spiritual life, not the
search for a magnified tranquillizer. Healthy prayer is
born from the desire of being with God, not from the
compulsive need of an infallible psychiatrist.

If our prayers are always imperious demands for help, then we have slipped into neurotic praying. Why have I said 'always'? It quite frequently happens that a person's first contact with God takes on this form of urgent need. And in times of difficulty, sickness and emotional suffering, it is right that we seek the Lord in this way. Many people of God began their journey of faith when going through a deep crisis! Need is often the Holy Spirit's alarm clock that leads us to God, and this is a legitimate door to faith. This type of prayer is acceptable at an initial stage. But it ought to give way to a much more mature relationship: we cannot reduce God to a mere psychiatrist or prayer to an aspirin. Otherwise, as soon as the headache – the need – disappears, any spirituality will also fade away. It is a faith that melts away: a pseudo-spirituality that is born out of an egotistical desire – although natural – to receive a powerful source of help.

This possibly explains why certain people abandon the faith or the church after a period of time. They no longer need their God. Their fleeting faith was the result of psychological projections. As soon as the problem was solved, they left the Lord. In these cases we have to recognise the justice of Freudian psychoanalytic criticism. For this type of person, God has not been more than an expression of their desires. If God is not more than an errand runner, a good fairy godmother, this is an unbalanced type of prayer and spirituality and, therefore, we are standing on quicksand. Our life of faith cannot be so primary and instinctive as that of the immature young fellow who said, 'When I cannot do anything more, then I have two recourses left: to cry and to pray.' So, prayer is a 'last recourse'!

In the previous chapter we have already seen how request forms an integral and legitimate part of prayer.

But we cannot confuse the benefits with the purpose. We do not pray, first of all, to feel peace, or to have joy, or to avoid loneliness. All of this is a result of prayer, but not its reason for being. When a believer sees prayer only or primarily the instrument by which to obtain things from God, they have not understood the very essence of prayer.

After considering these implications, let us analyse the therapeutic effects of prayer.

Prayer as an existential therapy

The therapeutic value of prayer is not limited to the psychological effects that I will mention later on. In addition to its restorative power on the emotions, prayer has a profound existential dimension that comes even before its therapeutic capacity. By existential, I mean all the questions about the real meaning of our life: what am I here for? Where do I come from? Is there any hope after life is over? For us, this existential aspect comes before any other because its consequences are much more long lasting and serious. This is why we must begin our description of the healthy effects of prayer on this point.

Certain modern schools of psychotherapy, the so-called existential schools, maintain that man's central problem lies in his lack of meaning in life. Authors such as Victor Frankl[4] and Binswanger identify a person's basic problem as the lack of vital meaning with its inevitable results: desperation, the sense of cosmic disorientation, the nausea of which Sartre speaks.[5] The solution, they believe, lies in finding significant and enriching relationships. Man's therapeutic key is to be found in encounters with others: a genuine relationship is the main healing instrument.

This viewpoint of the existential schools partially coincides with the biblical diagnosis of human nature. God created humans with their greatest need being the need for relationships. 'It is not good that man should be alone, I will make him a helper fit for him' said God, from the very beginning (Gen. 2:18). This ought not to surprise us since humans were made in the image and likeness of their Creator who, from eternity, enjoys a harmonious and intimate relationship among the persons of the Trinity. This helps us understand that human beings are born with that profound need of having contact with a 'you'.

These relationships are two-dimensional: with our fellow human beings there is the horizontal dimension; but also there is the vertical dimension, with our Creator. Such was man's original situation, as biblical truth describes it to us. The most vital relationship is the relationship with our Creator. In Genesis chapters 1 and 2, human beings did not have emotional problems: there was no fear, no shame and no pain, because there was a perfect relationship between God and man, and that gave total fulfilment. For this reason the separation from God is the deepest source of neurosis, because our deepest need is not being met. Jung himself, in a very famous quotation, said that 'I have never seen a single case of neurosis that ultimately did not have an existential origin.' This existential loneliness and lack of meaning is sometimes terrible to experience. Jesus' words on the cross: 'My God, my God, why have you forsaken me?' remind us of the intense pain of this reality. How right were the Spanish mystic authors of the sixteenth century, St John of the Cross and Teresa de Avila, when they wrote about 'the dark night of the soul without God'. Yes, being away from God is a terrible experience, probably the most disturbing any human being can ever face. This is Hell – not being able to have that relationship with God.

It is precisely here where the great therapeutic power of prayer enters into the scene. Inasmuch as it is fellowship with God, prayer is a return to the first relationship, with the obvious limitations imposed upon us by our fallen nature, the limitations that I considered in detail in chapters 1 and 2.

Prayer enables us to rebuild the very foundations of our existence, and gives back to a person the true purpose of their life: relationship with God. It provides an authentic self-fulfilment because it restores free and constant dialogue, that intimate fellowship with our Creator. Prayer is the vehicle that allows us to meet our deepest need, our thirst for God. Thus, I affirm that it contains a very significant therapeutic element for which there is no substitute. It is not enough to give people rich relationships with their fellows. It is for these reasons that I am convinced that prayer contains the therapeutic key par excellence: it gives meaning to our existence. Or in other words, it fills that 'void that has the shape of God' that only God can fill. Herein lies the first and most profound therapeutic effect of prayer. The Psalmist expressed the same idea with great poetical force: 'As the deer pants for streams of water, so my soul pants for you, O God. My soul thirsts for God, for the living God' (Ps. 42:1–2).

Prayer as a psychotherapeutic process

We are now ready to examine the positive consequences of prayer from an emotional point of view. If we understand prayer as a personal relationship with God, a communication that is both rich and deep in its significance, its effects will hold a certain parallel to the consequen-ces of an effective psychotherapeutic relationship. By psychotherapy, I mean a way to treat emotional problems in which the main tool to promote healing is communication, either verbal or non-verbal, between the therapist and the patient. As in any long term psychotherapeutic process, there will be four positive results of prayer:

- an intimate relationship
- an unburdening – a catharsis
- guidance
- growth

Actually, within every fruitful relationship, within each true encounter between two people, these emotional phenomena appear. And much more here in prayer, where two unique realities are given: the therapist – God – is the Prince of Counsellors, the Physician par excellence, the Comforter. And the patient – each and every believer – has this intimate, internal Counsellor. In this specific aspect, prayer is a very special form of psychotherapy. Prayer leads to the emotional benefits of a deeply committed relationship and gives way to the emotional results proper to a deeply committed interaction. It is encouraging to see here how science and faith are not in contradiction, to discover how science's contributions – in this case, of psychology – do not contradict the spiritual realities but also fully confirm them. From the emotional point of view, prayer is the perfected reflection or echo of a deep therapeutic relationship.

I shall now examine these emotional effects that produce so much good for the believer.

An Intimate Relationship

Prayer gives us an emotional and spiritual warmth that is the result of an intimate contact with the Lord. It

comes from the genuine encounter, the mutual commitment of two people. In psychology we would speak of
an adequate rapport, and in psychoanalysis of a positive
transference. It is a feeling of harmony, of reciprocal
commitment, or intimacy. We all need to feel love, and
love is the result of an intimate relationship – and this is
exactly what God gives us.

It is within prayer that we experience that God is for
us, with us, and in us (cf. Eph. 4:6). Expressing this in
more academic terms, it is there that we experience
God's sympathy and empathy. We sense that we are
deeply understood because the one we are dialoguing
with, the Lord, is not someone remote from us, to be
found far away in the celestial regions, but 'one who has
been tempted in every way, just as we are – yet was
without sin' (Heb. 4:15). For this reason he can 'sympa-
thise with our weaknesses'. Although we do not see
him, we know that God is present because, thanks to the
reality of the Holy Spirit, God lives inside each of us.
And this is what allows us to come near to his presence
'with confidence, so that we may receive mercy and find
grace to help us in our time of need' (Heb. 4:16).

An expert psychotherapist has this to say: 'There cannot be any doubt that the relationship of the patient with
the therapist contains the strongest forces of the therapeutic venture. Changes always occur within the context
of an interpersonal relationship.' How is this produced
through the practice of prayer? In a strict sense, to pray
is to talk with God. But can we limit the concept of
prayer to this restricted idea of verbal communication?
If prayer, above all, is dialogue with God, the essential
requisite for dialogue is communication. All productive
dialogue includes much more than words. Words are a
beautiful instrument within a relationship, but are not
the only element and not even the most important.

Someone has already said that 'words are silver, but silence is golden'. Indeed there can be a tremendous amount of communication with very few words. And the opposite is also true. Two people can speak together for hours using a multitude of words but without any true communication. (This is what someone has termed a 'duelogue', that is, two people speaking, but none listening!)

Something similar happens in our communication with God. We cannot limit the concept of prayer to words, no matter how important the words may seem. Talking with God is only one of the dimensions of this dialogue, in the same way that verbalization is only one of the facets of communication. There exists an unspoken language: the language of intention, of desire, of the heart. We see this very thing in daily life. The husband – or vice versa – can transmit much to his wife even if he speaks very little, because there is a type of dialogue that is non-verbal, that involves gestures of tenderness, a loving look, positive attitudes, a dialogue whose rich shades and dimensions escape the realm of words. So we cannot impoverish prayer, limiting it exclusively to verbal communication.

This concept, prayer without words, brings us into a very rich terrain that is nonetheless not exempt from danger. In the final chapter I will try to analyse the dangers that come from reducing Christian prayer to a form of Eastern mysticism, of meditation void of content, of vague silence centred upon oneself.

But let us now examine this intimate relationship in detail: what are these aspects of our non-verbal communication with the Lord? If we agree that the Christian's life is, first of all, a personal relationship, we will do well to remember in what terms God understands this relationship. To do so, we will use the analogy that the Lord himself used in speaking with his own people, both in the Old and New Testaments: the love in a couple's relationship, marital love. 'As a bridegroom rejoices over his bride, so wilt your God rejoice over you' (Is. 62:5). Paul's epistle to the Ephesians (Eph. 5:23–30) brings before us the same reality: the genuine love of Christ for his Bride, the church.

In a love relationship, the communication form par excellence is being close to or alongside the loved one. If the relationship that the Lord wants of us is to be characterized by love for him, then first of all we need to practise being in his presence. This is the idea that appears so often throughout the Psalms. David sums it up beautifully in Psalm 27:4, 'One thing I ask of the Lord, this is what I seek: that I may dwell in the house of the Lord all the days of my life.' Psalm 84:1–2 reads, 'How lovely is your dwelling place, O Lord Almighty! My soul yearns, even faints for the courts of the Lord.' The key is 'to be with' or 'to be in'. This is the first and indispensable requisite for a love relationship to be able to grow. Without the presence of the loved one, no intimacy is possible, and without intimacy, there can be no progress in the relationship. It is important to note how in the Old Testament and especially in the Psalms, the idea of prayer is inseparably joined to the concepts of intimate communion and meditation; they are like a bunch of grapes, where it is difficult to distinguish where the various smaller clusters begin and end.

On occasion, a husband, bogged down with a thousand preoccupations, develops guilt feelings for not dedicating enough time to his wife. To make up for this, he gives her things – today a bouquet of flowers, tomorrow a box of chocolates ... This is not wrong and the wife should not reject these demonstrations of affection. But the gifts can never be a substitute for the centre of their relationship: being together, spending time at each other's side. Something similar sometimes happens in our Christian life. We do so many things for God that we do not have enough time to be with him. We work so hard in the work of the Lord that there is no place for the Lord of the work. Be aware of activism! We can bring many gifts to the Lord, immersed in a thousand spiritual activities, but deep down these are all a mere imitation of true love. It is difficult for us to understand it, and it even surprises us, but God does want to be with us. The Lord is delighted when his children seek him. God is self-sufficient, he has need of nothing; nonetheless, he takes great pleasure in our relationship with him, in our prayers.

To be close to the one we love is a vital communication form. This attitude transmits a message that cannot be substituted: 'I want to be with you because you are important to me; it does me good to be by your side.' This is the communication by gestures that produces a form of dialogue, without words, but equally significant. The Lord seeks worshippers who 'will worship the Father in spirit and truth' (Jn. 4:23). To come near unto God, to be with him, giving him an unequivocal sign of our love with our presence, is in itself a form of prayer. 'Lord, this time is yours; here I am, speak to me as you want.'

Along this line, the French doctor and Nobel Prize winner, Alexis Carrel, expresses the same idea with great literary beauty: 'Through prayer, man offers himself to God like the canvas before the painter or the marble before the sculptor.'[6]

Even though our words may be few and awkward, even though we may not feel the presence of the Beloved at our side, to be with him is a form of prayer that satisfies God and, therefore, ought to satisfy us as well. This is where the importance of discipline comes in, as was pointed out in chapter 2. Choosing to seek God in prayer pleases him greatly, regardless of our feelings. To have the desire to pray and to make the decision to pray is already an obedience that glorifies the Lord. Remember that the will is no less important than thoughts or feelings. The determined decision to set aside a specific time for the Lord and to meet it resolutely is something truly valuable.

This analogy of conjugal love takes us to a second consideration. The benefit that we can obtain from this relationship is not the prime reason for being next to our partner. The first purpose of prayer is not for it to do something good to us. Even though this would be legitimate, it is a consequence. But it is not its *raison d'être* nor does it always happen. The first purpose of prayer is to promote a deep communication and the growth of our relationship with God. We do not pray *for*, we pray *because*. We do not have the right to seek first our own good when we pray. This is an egocentric focus that is seen as often in the prayer life as in the love relationship of many couples.

We must recognize and confess that many of us force our prayer life to revolve around us and not around our God. We are egotistical, without realising it, even in this spiritual activity par excellence. Where is God left in such prayer? Do we care about what he feels and thinks? Or are we only concerned for ourselves? It sometimes seems as if we are the only thing that matters in prayer. This conduct can be observed in an attitude that is frequently seen: we measure the quality of our prayer by how we feel once we have finished praying. If I feel good, prayer has been successful. Otherwise, I have failed. This way of thinking, apart from placing the emphasis where it does not belong – on feelings – loses sight of the central purpose of prayer. The centre of prayer ought to be God himself. Sometimes even very spiritual activities can hide pockets of egoism. More frequently, the question we ought to ask when we finish praying is, 'What does God think?' and not, 'How do I feel?' He is our Lover and lovers are happy with the presence of the loved one.

Prayer, just as in a love relationship, implies giving – and giving of ourselves. Someone has compared it to a plant that one must water regularly and look after in the way that a living organism requires. Otherwise, it will wither. The same thing happens with our personal relationship with God: if we do not cultivate it and give it careful attention, we will only end up with drought and frustration. Prayer is one of the basic instruments needed to 'water' our relationship with God; possibly the instrument par excellence. That is why to be with God, to breathe in his presence through prayer, is not as much an end in itself but the means by which this personal relationship with him can grow.

To summarise what I have discussed so far:

- Prayer is more than talking with God, it is daily practising the presence of God in our lives through a dialogue that is open to all communication, both verbal and non-verbal.
- The centre of prayer should not be ourselves but the Lord. Our prayers should be theocentric, not egocentric.
- Prayer is not an end in itself, but a means by which the presence of God can be breathed and by which our living relationship with him can be fed.

Understood in this fashion, prayer will be more a pleasure than an obligation. In a society that is so full of responsibilities, our life of prayer ought not become one more burden. Of course it implies some struggle and discipline. But it is also an oasis of peace where I experience the intimate and personal love of God.

Nevertheless, here we also find difficult ground. To the problems mentioned in chapter 2 are now added those dealing with this relational aspect of prayer. Why is this? A relationship is not as simple as it seems. From the psychological point of view, it becomes a complex and delicate process influenced by the factors from our past and from our unconscious that I have already mentioned.

In fact, the more intimate a relationship, the more complex. This is why in every intimate relationship unexpected reactions surface that one does not fully understand. They are unwanted and surprising feelings, almost incomprehensible, that make more difficult the process of coming closer. These reactions are known in psychology as transference. In a few words, this phenomenon consists in the repetition – as if they were an echo – of the problems experienced during childhood. This primarily takes place in those situations where elements of authority or love exist. We transfer (this is where the term comes from) the relationship problems we had with our first authority and love figures, our father and mother, to our present circumstances. And since our relationship with God, as was discussed in the previous chapter, presents certain echoes of that paternal–child relationship, we have a field that is fertile for obstacles.

As a result, the difficulty in a relationship with God can be the partial expression of a deeper problem: the difficulty of developing relationships in general. A young person commented to me, 'I feel uncomfortable in all my relationships, not only with God. I always feel displaced, but this is felt even more strongly in prayer.' Generally, if someone finds all relationships difficult to develop, they will feel uneasy, almost anxious after praying. They will suffer from a mixture of impotence and imperfection: 'I have the impression that I've done things all wrong, that I've done terribly. I haven't praised the Lord with the intensity that I wanted. I haven't worshipped him with the fervour that he deserves. I believe that I'm forgetting something that I ought to be thankful for.'

I need to make three observations regarding this point:

First of all, the origin of an inability to form and sustain relationships normally lies in a defective self-esteem, in the lack of confidence in oneself. I will return to this issue of self-esteem at the end of the chapter because it also has dangers if it is unduly emphasised outside its proper biblical framework, but we must say here that the necessary requisite for us to be able to approach others adequately is a healthy concept of personal identity. The development of intimacy in relationships will depend upon the security that one has in oneself. The more unsure a person is, the more relational conflicts the person will have. The poorer the person's self-image, the greater the difficulty in becoming close to others. Deep down, people who have relational problems with others have not learned to relate well to themselves. They are in conflict with others because of the conflict with themselves.

The result of all this will be problems in having an intimate relationship with God. They will find it difficult to trust in God because it is difficult for them to trust in themselves. Their fear of getting hurt will lead them to adopt a defensive attitude. Later on, the same young person said, 'My problems with prayer were a reflection of my problems with God, and my problems with God were problems that I had with myself. Their cause did not lie in God, nor in our relationship, but in me.'

When we are in this situation it is easy to enter a vicious circle. On the one hand we know that a healthy personal identity ought to be nourished by God. As believers, our inner security does not depend – in the last analysis – on what we think about ourselves, but on what God says that he thinks about us. Incidentally, this is a very therapeutic point of the gospel message. But, on the other hand, how do we experience this if it is precisely our relationship with God that is blocked by the emotional problem? It is here where we find a good example of the possible collaboration between psychology and faith. The work of a good counsellor who goes about clarifying these inner conflicts, together with the enlightening work of the Holy Spirit, can be enormously therapeutic. It is a complementary process that is developed, like a feedback mechanism: the spiritual action helps the psychological, and vice versa.

Second, the dissatisfaction we feel after praying does not necessarily reflect a prayer that is poor in quality or low in fervency. Far from this, it can be a sign of spiritual maturity. It may not reveal poverty but the sensitivity and consciousness of sin that the Holy Spirit puts inside us. I will expand on this subject later on. For now, let me say only that our subjective feelings of imperfection do not necessarily correspond with God's opinion. We sometimes judge ourselves with greater severity than the Lord does. But, if we remember the wide framework of prayer as a relationship, we will better understand the relative importance of the results. To make the decision to pray is already of value in itself. I can have a feeling of failure in the area of praise or of confession. It may be that on a particular day my spirit is low and the form that my prayers take is dead. But when I say to God, 'Lord, I want to draw near unto you with all my heart and this time belongs to you', this attitude in itself is already a prayer. Its success does not depend on my verbal communication but on my attitude. Yes, in prayer, the heart is as important as the words. Let us also remember that our clumsy verbal expression does not keep God from understanding our prayer, since, 'Before a word is on my tongue, you know it completely, O Lord' (Ps. 139:4).

Let us imagine, nonetheless, that our feelings of frustration are due to some deficiency on our part and that our prayers are, in fact, weak. This brings us to the third consideration: God sees our prayers with the eyes of grace; they reach him by the merits of Christ, not by our own. God's acceptance of our prayer does not depend on how well or how poorly we pray, but on the Lord's grace. If not, what meaning do those brief expressions have with which we end our prayers? 'In the name of Jesus Christ', and 'by Christ's merits' are not just rituals, empty phrases. They are the theological key that enables us to come near to God, freed from the tyranny of having to please him.

We sometimes see prayer as if it were a kind of examination: 'How have I done? Well or badly? What grade is the Lord going to give me?' This way of thinking, even if it is unconscious, eventually transforms the life of prayer into a heavy burden. We think our way of praying ought to please the Lord because, if not, he will not listen to us. Of course the form is important. Our prayers ought to be respectful, fervent, persevering. We find enough teaching on this in the epistles not to minimize this aspect. But we should not associate the form of praying with the attention that God gives to that prayer. By being able to add 'by the merits of Christ', our prayers reach the Lord in perfect shape. This frees us from seeing each prayer as a test. The theological principle of grace is also applied here. Woe to us if the Lord were to evaluate our Christian conduct on the basis of our own merits! God sees our life in its entirety, including prayer, through the eyes of grace.

Also on this point, we can discover deep psychological problems. The person constantly at war with themselves, because of a lack of self-acceptance. This person's report card will read, 'I'm never happy; I can always do better.' This kind of perfectionism springs from a devalued self-image and self-appreciation. This person's security depends constantly on the opinion of other people. Their Christian life is tormented by feelings of permanent insecurity regarding God: the person knows that they are clean but does not feel clean, and this makes their prayer time more a demonstration of the fight within themselves. Since their life is a permanent difficulty, prayer is also a continuous problem. Their self-examination will always prove negative. The rejection of their own personality makes them feel unworthy, not so much morally as emotionally. 'I could not approach God and enter into his presence because I didn't feel clean, justified, through Christ. The basic problem was that I was harshly rejecting myself.' 'Nothing that I did seemed right. Everything seemed too little, insufficient: I was a slave to a neurotic perfectionism.' 'My praying was a constant struggle to feel accepted by the Lord. He had already accepted me a long time before. The problem was in me!' For this reason they will need to cling, more than anyone else, to the liberating grace of Christ.

In this context, what a consolation is the text of Revelation 5:8! Each of the four living creatures had 'golden bowls full of incense, which are the prayers of the saints'. Prayers are considered 'golden bowls' because they are wrapped in the grace of Christ. There is only one condition: they must come from the saints and we know from the New Testament that every believer is a saint in the eyes of God (see 1 Peter 2:9 and many other verses). For God it is not important so much how we pray as who prays.

We find a similar idea in the book of Proverbs, 'The prayer of the upright pleases him' (Prov. 15:8b). The content and the form, even though they are important, remain on a secondary level. The author of the prayer is always the most important. God's target has always been the heart. We must try to ensure that our praying is correct in form and balanced in content. But our first concern ought to be a spirit of holiness and uprightness in our personal lives. The key evaluating question ought not to be, 'What is my prayer like?' but 'What am I like?'

This brings us in naturally to consider the second therapeutic consequence of prayer from an emotional point of view.

Liberation

Pour out your hearts to him, for God is our refuge.

(Ps. 62:8)

Prayer is an excellent vehicle of expression, of unleashing our feelings, our problems and all our oppressions. In psychological terms, we speak about the cathartic value of prayer. Catharsis means to freely pour out, without any restrictions whatsoever, all that we feel or think. This free expression of our emotions or thoughts has a purifying effect (in the original Greek, the word 'catharsis' means purging, cleanliness).

This kind of prayer is frequently found in the Psalms, especially those written by David, who used to pour out all his anguish to God. But the climax is again in the life of our Master. The Lord Jesus Christ knew the renovating effect of prayer well. After a tiring day, weighed down by hard work and temptation, he sought rest in his relationship with the Father (Mt.14:3). The same thing happens when the intensity of the ministry became almost feverish (Lk. 5:15–16). Similar situations occur in Mark 1:35 and other Gospel passages. For the Lord, prayer was the vehicle of rest par excellence. But let's go back again to Jesus' prayer in Gethsemane (Mt. 26). We find here the most impressive passage in Scripture regarding prayer's liberating effects. In his memorable words we can clearly distinguish two parts: in the first – verses 37–38 – Jesus pours out his heart in deep anguish, expressing all the emotions and thoughts which so heavily grieved him: '… he began to be sorrowful and troubled … My soul is overwhelmed with sorrow.'

Although the word prayer is not explicitly mentioned here, the spirit of meditation and fellowship with the Father – 'keep watch with me' – clearly shows us an attitude of prayer. Jesus had not yet begun speaking directly to the Father – verse 39 – but he was, in fact, already praying. First he needed to empty his soul and share all the ominous feelings which tormented him. It is only after this cathartic expression that Jesus feels liberated to go on a step: 'Going a little farther …' Now Jesus is ready for a more formal prayer and he is able to 'fall with his face to the ground' with surprising serenity and pray: 'Father not my will, but yours. If it is possible …' The order of the events is therefore full of meaning: first, a time of intense struggle whose main feature is the expression of pain, then readiness for acceptance, submission, and inner peace in spite of turmoil. The first part of his prayer gave Jesus liberation; it was the clue which allowed him to 'move a step forward'. These are the liberating effects of prayer to the tormented person.

It is in this context that the words of Jesus in Matthew 11:28 reach their full significance, 'Come to me, all you who are weary and burdened, and I will give you rest.' Rest is a natural result of expression, of pouring everything out in prayer. For this same reason, the apostle Peter exhorts us to 'cast all your anxiety on him' (1 Pet. 5:7). Paul, in Philippians 4:6–7 talks about this liberating effect in terms of peace: 'Do not be anxious about anything, but in everything, by prayer and petition, with thanksgiving, present your requests to God. And the peace of God ... will guard your hearts.' As Darling, the Christian psychologist, says, 'through prayer, we feel a release of new life which renews our entire being'.[7] Be ready to unburden your heart before the Father, when you need to, as Jesus did. God will not rebuke you.

Not only is prayer a renovation in the sense of rest, but it is a stocking up of new strength. A natural consequence of rest is strengthening. Referring once more to the prayer in Gethsemane – a real gem in our subject – let us notice what Luke wrote at the end of the passage: 'an angel from Heaven ... strengthened him' (Lk. 22:43). This sentence, only used by Luke the physician, is the natural conclusion of the therapeutic value of prayer: new strength, inner renewal.

The French doctor mentioned earlier, Alexis Carrel, wrote in an article published in a Swiss magazine, 'Prayer is not only an act of worship, that is, the most powerful form of energy that can be stirred up ... Prayer is a force as real as universal gravitation ... In praying, we are joined to that inexhaustible driving force that makes the world turn.'[8]

Many centuries before Carrel, God's wisdom brought us a very similar idea through the prophet Isaiah, '(God) gives strength to the weary and increases the power of the weak ... those who hope in the Lord will renew their strength. They will soar on wings like eagles: they will run and not grow weary, they will walk and not be faint' (Is. 40:29,31).

One particular type of catharsis comes through confession. It is here where prayer probably reaches the high point of its therapeutic power. In this sense, Paul Tournier is quite brave when he affirms, 'The Christian confession leads to the same psychological liberation that the best psychoanalytical cures do.'[9] The therapeutic effect of confession is one of the greatest blessings that the believer can experience. To feel intensely God's forgiveness for a specific sin is an inimitable comfort. We read these words of David in Psalm 32, 'Then I acknowledged my sin to you and did not cover up my iniquity. I said, "I will confess my transgressions to the Lord" – and you forgave the guilt of my sin ... You are my hiding place; you will protect me from trouble and surround me with songs of deliverance' (vv. 5, 7). And especially in Psalm 51, 'Cleanse me with hyssop, and I will be clean; wash me, and I will be whiter than snow. Let me hear joy and gladness; let the bones you have crushed rejoice' (vv. 4,7–8). The natural consequence of confession is to experience joy and gladness, to feel oneself surrounded with songs of deliverance.

Some people, nonetheless, do not feel this relieving and soothing effect of confession, even though their prayer has been genuine. 'I know that God has forgiven me, but I do not feel it inside.' Why? The problem usually lies in the fact that, in spite of God's certain forgiveness, these individuals have not forgiven themselves. The sin they have committed has been so great an offence to their self-image, their self-love has been so deeply hurt, that they are incapable of forgiving themselves. This especially occurs in cases where the sin is sexual immorality. If there has been a genuine confession, but the person still feels guilty, we are probably facing a psychological problem. The inability to forgive oneself is an issue more related to our self-image than to our faith; the obstacle is not in our relationship with God but in the relationship with ourselves. To recognize this reality is to alleviate the anguish greatly. All sins can be forgiven, big or little, regardless of the damage they do to our self-image.

On occasion it may be necessary to confess the sins to someone else, a counsellor, pastor, or a close friend. It is not as much a matter of confessing to the other person as it is of confessing to God in the company of another person. This provides a very healthy amount of objectivity that contributes to dissipating psychological doubts, and this is lacking if we confess in silence, alone. In the Protestant camp we have reacted against the audible confession of sins for justifiable theological reasons. We ought to avoid falling into the opposite extreme, however, the complete rejection of any confession in the presence of another brother or sister. Confessing before someone who understands us is of tremendous therapeutic value, both psychologically and spiritually. This is explicitly mentioned in the letter of James: 'Therefore confess your sins to each other and pray for each other so that you may be healed. The prayer of a righteous man is powerful and effective' (Jas. 5:16). It is most striking to see the close relationship between these three realities: confession, prayer and healing. Having the three words together in the text provides us with a very meaningful reminder of the therapeutic value of confession and prayer. As Eugene Peterson writes – about the same verse – in his paraphrase of the New Testament, 'Confess your sins to each other and pray for each other so that you can live whole and healed.' These three things go together.

From the emotional point of view, this is important because the injuries heal over much more rapidly when someone intimately knows about our sin and has prayed with us and for us. Many patients have expressed their deep gratitude to me because in my office they have been able to open up their heart and pour out those secrets of their life that they had never before shared with anyone else. The tears shed in the company of another have a therapeutic potential far greater than the emotions expressed in solitude. Tears in solitude can become embittering to the soul, tears in company are almost always soothing to the broken heart.

Three practical recommendations must be made before concluding this point. They are very basic observations but are of great importance in a topic where maintaining confidentiality is as important as the one with which we are dealing:

● The confession made by a brother or sister in Christ should always be completely voluntary – never compulsory. We do not have the right to exert any pressure, of any type, to get the person to confess a sin to us. The use of manipulation to facilitate the 'forcing out' of the sin can produce adverse psychological effects as severe as those from rape. Privacy is the property of our neighbour and we do not have the right to enter unless the door is voluntarily opened to us. Following along this same line, it is of concern to see the ease – almost unconscious – with which certain believers, especially those belonging to the 'Healing of Past Memories' movement, force their entrance into others' privacy. Their work can be positive when the 'patient' is the one who takes the initiative to open the door of their heart. But there have been many cases of abuse in this technique: abuses carried out in the name of Christ or the Holy Spirit that bring about disastrous emotional consequences for the one suffering this invasion of privacy. God exhorts us to weep with those who weep; not to break and enter private dwellings.

● A sin's confession is always a secret: it is something strictly confidential. This seems to be simple enough: a secret is a secret. But, how many problems, how many broken relationships, how much tension, exist in the life of a local church or of a family that have come because someone did not know how to keep something so basic! When something is confided to us, not even those people closest to us – our partner – ought to know of it. The only exception is when we have the permission of the person involved. If we see the need to share the secret with our spouse, perhaps to unload it from ourselves, we can do so as long as the one who shared their secret has given us their consent. The book of Proverbs tells us, 'if you argue your case with a neighbour, do not betray another man's confidence' (Prov. 25:9). The person who does not know how to be faithful in small things – such as keeping a secret – will not be faithful in bigger things either.

● When someone has confessed a fault to us, it is recommended that we pray for the person in their presence and out loud. This adds a dimension of objectivity to the person's relationship with God that has a very positive effect as we just saw in James 5:16. In fact, one of the most received requests from Christians in similar situations is, 'Keep on praying for me.' It is a great relief to know that someone is concerned enough to pray for us after a fall.

Light, guidance and discernment

When we look at ourselves in the mirror of a dimly lit room, we cannot see our physical defects. The half light protects us from discovering the reality of the wrinkles, baldness and acne. We only have to turn on the light to confirm our true situation. Something similar happens in our relationship with God. As long as we compare ourselves to others, to the average believers in our church or country, it seems to us that we are not all that bad. The dim light alleviates our uneasiness and can even make us feel optimistic. But as soon as we find ourselves in God's presence, we begin to discover, one by one, the multitude of 'spiritual wrinkles' in our lives. God's presence, his holiness, that we are able to apprehend through prayer, if only in an imperfect manner, sheds light onto our spiritual reality. This is why the Psalmist asks the Lord to, 'Send forth your light and your truth, and let them guide me' (Ps. 43:3).

This is another of the great therapeutic benefits of prayer: the discernment we get regarding our selves and our faults. In psychological terms we would say that prayer facilitates introspection, or insight. Through prayer, we come to realise things. It is quite interesting to note the structure of Psalm 32, mentioned earlier. After the confession (vv. 5–7), we come upon an apparently unexpected verse, 'I will instruct you and teach you in the way you should go' (v. 8). But this ought not come as a surprise to us if we understand that God's guidance is a natural consequence of walking with him and breathing in his presence. How deep – from the psychological point of view – is David's prayer in another Psalm, 'I will praise the Lord, who counsels me: even at night my heart instructs me' (16:7). Or his confident statement about God's power to give light in our life, 'You, O Lord, keep my lamp burning: my God turns my darkness into light' (Ps. 18:28).

'That which is truly fertile in our dialogue with God are the questions that he asks us, not those that we ask him.'[10] Yes, through prayer, God uncovers those areas of our lives that need repairing or even radical surgery. It allows us to gain a wider understanding of ourselves with greater objectivity, advancing through the 'psychological underbrush' of our personality. Teresa of Avila said, 'The divine inner words are produced in the soul at moments when it is incapable of understanding them....'".[11] But little by little this understanding grows and God turns our darkness into light: 'For with you is the fountain of life; in your light we see light' (Ps. 36:9). This kind of introspection does not seek to delve into a labyrinth of inner feelings (see chapter 5). It is not an unceasing self-analysis in search of that panacea about ourselves. Its purpose is simpler: to uncover, to make known so as to correct. This was exactly the idea of the verse in Job 34:32, 'Teach me what I cannot see: if I have done wrong, I will not do so again.' God is willing to give us instruction through prayer – that is why it is so important to keep silent some of the time.

For this reason, many prayers go accompanied by a feeling of conviction of sin. This feeling is positive, because it reflects spiritual maturity. God speaks to us through his holiness and makes us see the sin in its generic sense or see specific sins in our life. This guilt feeling, at the same time, leads us to Christ in a renovated way. This is the struggle Paul describes in Romans chapter 7 when he uncovers 'bags' of moral impotence.

His feeling of a lack of dignity is so overwhelming that it leads him to exclaim, 'What a wretched man I am! Who will rescue me from this body of death?' (Rom. 7:24).

All of this leads to a greater maturity in our relationship with God and to a further enrichment of our faith. The most mature Christian is not the one who sins less, but the one who has a greater awareness of his sin and confesses it. Therefore, we are not to take as negative those feelings of unworthiness that invade us when we pray. The second Beatitude alludes to this fact. When we recognise our identity before God, we feel 'poor'. This makes us weep – the second Beatitude. But these are tears that reflect a deep spiritual sensitivity because they spring from our self-examination carried out before God's bright and shining holiness. Unamuno, a Spanish philosopher, was right when he wrote in his private diary, 'The tears of anguish irritate and excite; but those of repentance are the ones that wash.'[12]

Prayer, together with meditation, is one of the most powerful instruments that God can give to provide us with adequate spiritual self-knowledge. It frees us from our strong tendency to self-deception. David's prayer in Psalm 19 hits the mark when he says, 'Who can discern his errors? Forgive my hidden faults … may they not rule over me' (vv. 12–13). We all have a great tendency to self-deceive ourselves. The unbeliever does this because of his short-sightedness before spiritual realities (Rom. 1:21). But the believer is not freed either from the problem because the human heart is 'deceitful above all things' (Jer. 17:9). In psychoanalysis, this phenomenon is called denial. It is a very elementary psychological defence mechanism that protects us from those realities that are too hard or painful to accept. It is in these corners of darkness where God's light penetrates and transforms. Prayer is the eyewash that clears up our vision and enables us to perceive the reality about ourselves. It provides us with discernment regarding our faults and errors. Prayer is God's instrument to avoid a diagnosis as wrong as the one made by the Laodicean church and mentioned in Revelation chapter 3. That is why the Lord has to say to it, 'I counsel you to buy from me ... salve to put on your eyes, so you can see' (v. 18). As Mathieu, the French writer, has said, 'this feeling of guilt, of sin, is the higher form of knowledge'.

To conclude this section, I want to quote the Psalmist once again in a memorable prayer (Ps. 139). He knew, from personal experience, about this searching and clarifying power of God:

> O Lord, you have searched me and you know me. You know when I sit and when I rise: you perceive my thoughts from afar. You discern my going out and my lying down; you are familiar with all my ways ... Search me, O God, and know my heart; test me and know my anxious thoughts. See if there is any offensive way in me, and lead me in the way everlasting.
>
> (Ps. 139:1–3,23–24)

Change

In fourth and last place, God uses prayer to progressively mould us, to make us change or grow. Just as the potter manually shapes the clay, the Lord uses prayer to forge us into the image of Christ. In fact, this benefit is a natural consequence of the previous ones. If God gives us his personal love within an intimate relationship, he gives us rest and peace through our expression and confession; he gives us discernment regarding our own person, and places a conviction of sin within us; all of these therapeutic effects result in a transformation of the believer.

The theologian Richard Foster affirms this in his book, *Celebration of Discipline*. 'To pray is to change. Prayer is the central avenue God uses to transform us.'[13] We come here to one of the most neglected benefits of prayer. Many Christians want to use prayer to solve their problems. God, on the other hand, wants prayer to become a transforming agent in our life.

Now then, how is this phenomenon produced? We will understand it when we consider the goal of this change, '…admonishing and teaching everyone with all wisdom, so that we may present everyone perfect in Christ' (Col. 1:28). God's purpose for us is to conform us to the image of his Son Jesus Christ, that we might look more like him day after day. God is forging within us a moral character that reflects the character of Christ.

What role does prayer have in this forging process? Let us consider the logical interdependence of all these steps. If we want to look like someone, we have to know what that person is like. Therefore, we must know what God is like. And knowledge of God, just as in any relationship, is only obtained by way of personal contact. The greater the intimacy, the better we know him. And this fellowship with God is basically obtained through prayer, together with the study of his word. In this aspect, prayer fulfils a central purpose in the Christian life: it makes possible our progressive likening to the image of Christ. As Christians, this is an essential goal in life.

Keeping this goal clearly in mind is very important in a society obsessed with the self. Many today make self-esteem the goal of psychological health. 'If you have good self-esteem, then you are a healthy person.' Selfism is a modern form of idolatry, to a point where we seem to live in the 'Me' generation. I cannot make a deep analysis of this phenomenon here – that would require another book! But I want to emphasize some basic ideas: a good self-image is an excellent way to glorify God because we are to love and affirm those aspects of our person which were made in the image of God (Eph. 2:10). The concern for our identity and self-esteem becomes a sin when we put our self first and God in second place. This is simply idolatry. Our goal in life is not self-fulfilment but Christ being magnified in us (Phil. 1:20). Our calling to self-denial is not a matter of insulting our person but of loving Christ. Self-denial means putting Christ first and everything else second. And certainly this is not incompatible with our efforts to improve our identity in all its dimensions – emotional, spiritual, or whatever.

After examining the therapeutic consequences of prayer, there is one question that probably comes up in many people's minds: What place does prayer occupy in psychotherapy, within a professional context? Can a Christian psychologist use prayer directly with their patients? And, what can the patient expect from prayer? This takes us briefly to our last consideration.

The use of prayer as therapy

Many Christian psychologists and psychotherapists consider prayer to be a valid resource in their work. As we have seen, it is an appropriate medium to bring about change and growth. Distinguished Christian professionals, such as H. Clinebell, Gary Collins, Larry Crabb, Paul Tournier and many others, frequently mention in their books the experience that they have had in this area. They, just as we, see no significant reason for ignoring the extraordinary therapeutic potential of prayer in their professional practice. Nevertheless, we will do well to bear in mind a couple of observations. In this context, prayer is a delicate instrument that must be used in a balanced and careful fashion. If we use it lightly and in an irresponsible way, it can do more harm than good. In the light of our professional experience, we can affirm that the use of prayer in psychotherapy becomes something much like a surgeon's scalpel: its therapeutic potential is extraordinary, but it must be handled wisely and with precision. Used incorrectly, it can awaken in the patient expectations that are not very realistic. If these hopes are not met they feel disappointed and begin to doubt, not only about prayer but about their faith. In some cases it can even cause resentment against God and bring about a process of spiritual coldness.

The apostle Paul made use of prayer to achieve something he really wanted: the elimination of his thorn in the flesh. And he prayed three times. We can imagine that he prayed with an intense faith, with his entire heart. But his desire was not fulfilled. The Lord's answer was quite clear: no, 'for my power is made perfect in weakness' (2 Cor. 12:9). The reason for this denial is not found in a lack of faith, nor in an ambiguous prayer, nor in a lukewarm spirituality on the part of the apostle. The reason was simply that God had other purposes.

It is legitimate to use prayer as a helping agent, something like a catalyst. But we cannot assume that God is going to say 'Yes' to all our prayers, or that a negative answer from the Lord is due to a lack of faith on our part. God is sovereign and he will not grant all our requests. We sometimes do not understand why God says 'No' or why certain things happen despite our prayers. But this should never be an excuse to say, 'I do not understand therefore I do not accept.' Paul in the passage above gives us the key attitude in these situations: contentment and acceptance. He says, 'For I have learnt to be content whatever the circumstances' (Phil. 4:11). When you feel disappointed with God's silence or refusals, say to him, 'Father, you know better than I. My vision is very limited, you see the overall picture of my life. I trust you.' It is far from my intention to simplify a very complex issue, but ultimately we must remember the words of Jesus to Peter: 'You do not realise now what I am doing, but later you will understand' (Jn. 13:7).

Second, prayer ought not be a substitute for other forms of help, professional or not. The approach of some believers is: 'If you have prayer, you do not need anything else; you can do everything through prayer. You do not need psychologists or doctors because God is the best psychologist and prayer is the best therapy.' They make a disjunctive consideration: 'either prayer or human science', as if both were incompatible with each other. This argument, unfortunately quite frequent, forgets that God has always used, as he uses today, human instruments guided by his Holy Spirit to bring peace and health to many people. God has a great variety of resources – human and divine – that he uses in his providence. To despise these helping instruments can be offensive, not only to God's servants, but also to God himself.

Prayer does not operate instead of but together with or alongside of. Actually, prayer is higher, it goes far beyond all of this: it must envelop everything. This is why the use of prayer is compatible with other therapeutic agents.

QUESTIONS AND ANSWERS:

These are some of the questions that have come as a result of this material being taught at Spring Harvest, based on the subjects that have been covered in the first three chapters of the book.

1 I have a tendency to pick up on other people's pain while praying for them, and then have to try to cope with it and to pray it out again. Is this a spiritual or a psychological problem?

If you are a good intercessor, you will experience compassion and sympathy for those you pray for – and sympathy makes you suffer. There are no easy answers – there is no way of avoiding suffering when you identify with those who suffer. People often ask me – as a professional psychiatrist – 'What do you do when you get home, to forget all the problems you hear in your office? How can you disconnect?' My answer is that there have been many sleepless nights and if you are a sensitive person who identifies with others, some suffering is unavoidable. Professionally you put certain ways to protect yourself – but I often say that when I started practising psychiatry, I weighed more!

A few practical suggestions may be helpful here:

- Remember that God cares for this person more than you or I do. If you are worried about them, realize that God, the supreme Pastor, is also concerned. Remember that the ultimate responsibility for a person's situation is God's, not ours. We are only God's fellow-workers (1 Cor. 3:9), but the architect is God. I always found this thought a great relief in my professional experience.

- If you need to share the burden with someone else, do it. It will help you to see the situation more objectively and thus to feel less weighed down. But be very careful to keep the confidentiality if this was required. Keeping a secret is a basic ingredient for mutual trust.

2 Where do feeling types come in prayer and intercession?

In the middle – they are neither the best nor the worst. They are usually very balanced and the only danger for them can be that they lack the discipline and method which is advisable in intercession. On the other hand, their capacity to identify with and care for those in need is an excellent treasure that they can use in intercession. The main danger for the feeling type in prayer is putting too much emphasis on the need to feel God near all the time. This mistake can turn their prayer life into an unbearable sequence of ups and downs.

3 How far do we have the right as Christians to ask specifically for what we want in prayer?

God is pleased, in general, for us to ask specifically and the more specific we are, the better. God likes us to be concrete in our requests. This is not always possible but remember Abraham's prayer: he bargained with God in a detailed way. God does not always answer our speci-fic prayers – sometimes he answers in different ways and at other times. God's calendar is not ours and sometimes we ask God for something and the answer may not come until years later – and what we wanted was an immediate answer. The Psalmist is very emphatic when he states: 'Delight yourself in the Lord and he will give you the desires of your heart' (Ps. 37:4). Because God is a loving Father, he wants the best things for his children: 'I will do whatever you ask in my name ... my Father will give you whatever you ask in my name' (Jn. 14:13; 16:23). So we do have the right to ask the Father for specific requests.

4 How can we be sure our specific requests are in line with God's will?

There is no definitive, certain way to know God's will in each specific area of our life, but we do have a general framework, a road map, which shows us very clearly what God wants and what he dislikes for our life. This general guidance should mould our requests: 'If you remain in me and my words remain in you, ask what-ever you wish, and it will be given you' said the Lord in John 15:7.

Sometimes, nonetheless, the only way to find it out is to try it: start walking. Step by step, little by little, you will find out if you are walking in the right way. The assurance we have is that when we walk wholeheart-edly before the Lord, he will not let us make any irre-versible mistakes. The promise in Psalm 37:23–24 is most encouraging; 'If the Lord delights in a man's way, he will make his steps firm; though he stumble, he will not fall, for the Lord upholds him with his hand'. The Lord holds our hand even when we make mistakes, provided we have the same attitude of the Psalmist in Psalm 25: obe-dience. This Psalm speaks very clearly on this subject. Try it: if it is not God's will, he will show it to you.

5 I am having problems forgiving someone who has really hurt me.

Forgiveness is never instantaneous. The willingness to forgive is immediate but the process of forgiving takes time. It may take years to forgive the one who has injured you and that is normal, because forgiving involves transforming open wounds into closed scars. Remember Joseph in Genesis – two or three years, if not more, elapses between when he first met his brothers again in Egypt and when he actually tells them who he was. Dietrich Bonhoeffer wrote of a cheap grace: I think we should also be wary of cheap forgiveness.

Forgiveness is not the same as forgetting. Actually to forget in a literal sense is impossible because we all have a memory of past events. The only one who is able to forgive and forget is God because he is out of time. But a memory can be stored in our minds in two different ways: either full of resentment and hostility, or with its negative emotions removed. Forgiveness requires us to empty the memory of its poison.

Nor does forgiveness necessarily involve going to the person who has injured you – but it does involve talking to God. When Jesus was on the cross, he prayed, 'Father, forgive them – they don't know what they are doing.' He didn't go to be reconciled to the people involved. Forgiveness is possible even if there is no reconciliation.

6 Where can people go for help if they have bad thoughts when they are praying?

If having bad thoughts makes you suffer a lot, you should go for counselling, and this is available on three levels:

- Pastorally: the church is a supporting community and the first step should be to talk to your minister or someone who is mature in the faith in your church.
- If this is not enough, try for counselling, which is usually practised by lay people who have had some train-

ing, not professionals. These are not qualified psychologists but they can be very helpful.

- If this is not enough still, then and only then should
  you go to the professional level; a psychiatrist or a
  psychologist. I would suggest that this professional
  should, in this case, be a Christian, otherwise if
  you say 'I have bad thoughts when I pray', they are
  likely to suggest solving the problem by not praying
  at all!

7 Can you say a bit more about depressives?

A depressive character or personality is a person who
has three problems:

- Everyone else is better than them – they have feelings
  of inferiority.
- They feel guilty about many things – because they
  feel insecure.
- They find it difficult to trust others because they have
  had an emotionally poor childhood. The bond of basic
  trust with their loved ones was not well developed.

These problems will have been long lasting, and gone on
for years, unlike depression itself, where similar symptoms occur for shorter and limited periods of time.

What can they do to improve?

They need to work out the subject of their identity. This
is a whole subject in itself, but some hints might help
them to start:

- They need to feel useful and creative – unemploy-
  ment threatens the identity. A sense of vocation, either

through paid work or on a voluntary basis, is essential to have a healthy identity.

- They need to develop relations – we all need to feel we belong, and church can be therapeutic here. Many identity problems arise from poor family relationships. The local church can give the opportunity to experience the shelter and warmth their lives have lacked.
- They need to have meaning in their lives and the gospel is very healing – it gives us a new perspective on our past and our future, new hope and new goals to live for. The depressive will say:

- I'm nobody
- I'm good for nothing
- I'm going nowhere

And the gospel answers:

- You're somebody in God's eyes
- You have something to do here
- You are going somewhere good

8 How can you stop yourself from being too introspective, constantly analysing things?

Some introspection may be helpful, as I have already pointed out. It is actually a fruitful way to start changes in our lives and personalities. 'Now, says the Lord, consider – or meditate – carefully your ways' (Hag. 1:7). This was a rather frequent exhortation to the people of Israel. But too much introspection leads to a spiritual and emotional desert because self-knowledge is ultimately disappointing and frustrating. Self-knowledge must always be balanced and enlightened by God's knowledge.

9 Where should I start if I want to improve emotionally?

The human personality has three parts: the will, which is expressed in decisions, the mind, which is expressed in the thoughts and the feelings, which are expressed in emotions. Since the fall, these three have been like animals which are difficult to train, and the most difficult to control are the feelings. So don't start with your feelings – start with your thoughts.

Put into practice what Paul said in 2 Corinthians 10:5 – 'Taking captive every thought in obedience to Christ.' This verse is actually the embryo of a type of psychotherapy – cognitive therapy – which is very much used today. It is amazing to realise how the biblical wisdom, in this case through Paul, anticipated modern psychology!

Thoughts are like seeds that eventually will bring forth feelings and decisions. So if you want to change any aspect of your personality start with your thoughts and the changes in your feelings will follow. But notice that 'taking captive' implies effort and even struggle. As Luther said, 'You cannot avoid the birds that fly over your head but you can prevent them from making a nest in your hair.'

1 V. Grounds, Emotional Problems and the Gospel (US: The Zondervan Corporation, 1976), p138

2 W. Oates, *The Religious Dimensions of Personality* (New York: Association Press, 1957)

3 A. Genis & M.A. Brun, *Más Allá de la Psiquiatría* [*Beyond Psychiatry*] (Buenos Aires: La Aurora, 1973)

4 V. Frankl, *Man's Search for Meaning* (Boston: Beacon Press, 1959)

5 J.P. Sartre, *La Náusea* (Buenos Aires: Losada, 1947), pp144, 176

6 A. Carrel, *La Incógnita del Hombre* (Ed. Joaquim Gil, Barcelona, 1942), p161

7 H.W. Darling, *Man in his Right Mind* (Carlisle: Paternoster Press, 1969), p140

8 A. Carrel, 'Le Pouvoir de la Prière', *Journal de Genève*, May 1940

9 P. Tournier, *Medicina de la Persona* (Pamplona: Editorial Gómez, 1965)

10 P. Tournier, *Medicina de la Persona* (Pamplona: Editorial Gómez, 1965) p317

11 Quoted by Paul Tournier in *Psychoanalytical Technique and Religious Faith* (Buenos Aires: La Aurora, 1969), p230

12 M. de Unamuno, Diario Intimo (Madrid: Alianza, 1973), p23

13 R. Foster, *Celebration of Discipline* (London: Hodder & Stoughton, 1980), p30

Part 2

The Apologetics of Prayer

Chapter 4

PRAYER – PSYCHOLOGICAL ILLUSION?

A psychiatrist's viewpoint

'Prayer is not real. It is purely a psychological phenomenon.' 'You're just imagining it: in reality you're speaking to a void, to a wall.' Or as a teenager might say, 'You've got your own thing going.' 'If I saw God here alongside me, then I'd pray. But this isn't anything more than a psychological trick.'

This way of thinking reflects the opinion of many people of our day. In chapter 5 I will examine the menace of syncretism, of having a pick'n'mix spirituality. But before that, I need to analyse the influence of another untouchable idol of our time, scientific materialism. We live in a generation that suffers from what has been termed 'the Thomas syndrome': 'If I don't see with my own eyes and touch with my own hands, I won't believe.'

Certain beliefs, which are psychologically based, have increasingly eroded the value of prayer in people's minds. These beliefs are held by many who have never studied the theories behind them.

Prayer is questioned, the spiritual reality of its meaning is denied, and even those that practise it come to be ridiculed. This is why I have dedicated an entire chapter to the apologetics of prayer from this psychological perspective. How can Christians respond to these attacks? The spiritual short-sightedness of our contemporaries ought not irritate us. On the contrary, it ought to awake in us a deep sense of compassion. But at the same time we must be capable of responding to their objections.

The Self-suggestion argument

Religion, in its diverse manifestations, has been associated with suggestion during many centuries. A good number of people see in religion, including its cardinal activity – prayer, a form of self-delusion. 'You believe that God is there and you imagine it, you convince yourself that it's like that.' Note the definition of suggestion: 'The acceptance or the effect of the statements or actions of one person upon another, depending on the emotional set-up of the recipient and his psychological relationship to the other person.'[1] In other words, when the mind accepts an idea as true, if this idea is reasonable, it lends to make itself real by way of unconscious processes. It would come to be the equivalent of the placebo effect in medicine. If I take a medicine that has nothing more than distilled water in it, but I believe it is a tranquillizer, it will, in effect, act as a sedative. Following this line, the Christian faith is presented as a form of suggestion.

What can we respond to this argument? We will consider three aspects that will help us to differentiate, as Christians, between suggestion and biblical faith:

The purpose of self-suggestion

The basic purpose of suggestion is always evasion. Escape
from a difficult reality is sought, whether this be a transitory circumstance or something much deeper, such as life
itself. In this case, religion would act as the great tranquillizer, the people's opium spoken of by Marx, to mitigate a
profound existential pain. It would be a supposedly transcendental escape that comes to satisfy our deepest needs.
Prayer is therefore the instrument par excellence, the best
medicine, to achieve this escapist effect.

Nonetheless, we find here the first contradiction.
When a Christian truly is following Christ, they choose
a way of evasion that does not come cheaply. Obedience
to the Lord is costly: it is a narrow path full of thorns.
Affliction, struggle, pain, and persecution often seem to
be the distinguishing mark of Christ's disciples. Of
course, this is not something that happens all the time to
every Christian, but some form of suffering seems quite
normal in the Christian life. We have only to read
Hebrews chapter 11 where it speaks about the other
heroes of the faith: 'Some faced jeers and flogging, while
still others were chained and put in prison. They were
stoned; they were sawed in two: they were put to death
by the sword. They went about in sheepskins and
goatskins, destitute, persecuted and mistreated' (Heb.
11:36–37). Some pleasant evasion! We could speak about
self-convincement and delusion if faith were to offer a
paradise on Earth. In that case it would act as an existential aspirin. But the Christian faith seems to be all to
the contrary: 'My peace I give unto you ... not as the
world gives it ... in the world you will be afflicted ...
because the servant is not greater than his Lord.'

This gives us two options: either all Christians are
masochists by nature, or else faith does not always help

us to evade reality. There are many more pleasant ways to escape! If the Christian faith were false, we would be dealing with a great fraud but not with an evasion of reality. Isn't it true that many believers would live with fewer preoccupations if they were not Christians? The level of personal peace, from a human point of view, quite often would be much higher without those problems that stem from a committed faith. 'Christ hasn't made my life easy. On the contrary, it would have been more comfortable to be without him than to live with him,' very accurately affirmed Dibelius, the Lutheran bishop.[2]

Faith can provide, and it does provide, a deep peace that stems from knowing a series of glorious realities. But it has never been the way of comfort or of evasion. Some years ago, an author, Emile Coué, expressed in the form of a slogan a popular definition of self-suggestion: 'Every day, I'm getting better in everything.'[3] What a contrast with the believer's experience! We can remember a declaration made by the apostle Paul: 'We are hard pressed on every side, but not crushed; perplexed, but not in despair: persecuted, but not abandoned; struck down, but not destroyed' (2 Cor. 4:8–9). Quite frankly, to explain the existence of Christianity in terms of self-suggestion implies an important lack of knowledge about its contents.

William James, in his classic book, *The Varieties of Religious Experience*, delves into the theme of human spiritual experience and affirms, among other things, 'The suggestive influence of ... environment plays an enormous part in all spiritual education. But the word "suggestion" is unfortunately beginning to play in many quarters the part of a wet blanket upon investigation, being used to fend off all inquiry.'[4] We cannot fall into the reductionism of putting everything religious into the box of self-suggestion.

The object of suggestion

People who are open to suggestion have certain characteristic personalities. We can note the definition that
appears in the prestigious book by Freedman and
Kaplan, one of the most authoritative voices in the psy-
chiatric field. 'Suggestibility is ... a state of uncritical
compliance with influence or uncritical acceptance of an
idea, belief or attitude. It is commonly observed among
people with hysterical traits.'[5] We have already dealt earlier with the first part of the definition. But, what about
the suggestibility – oriented personality? If suggestibility is intrinsic to hysterical personalities, what are the
psychological characteristics of hysterical personalities?
Consider the following carefully: 'The hysterical personality is dominated by the urgent need to please others ...
This results in restless activity, dramatization and exag-
geration, seductiveness, either social or overtly sexual ...
and immature and unrealistic dependence upon others.'[6]
But the description of this personality doesn't end here:
'The hysterical person, with his comedies, lies and con-
fabulations, does not cease to falsify his relationships
with others, always offers himself as a show, since his
very existence is, in his own eyes, a discontinuous series
of scenes and imaginary adventures.'[7]

Again, there is a dilemma here. We must choose between
two options: if a hysterical personality trait is required for
there to be suggestibility, then, either all Christians are hysterics, or the manifestations of faith are not necessarily an
exercise of suggestion. The logical argument is forceful. I do
not think anyone would dare affirm that all Christians are
hysterics! Thus, we must conclude that the faith, including
prayer, is not necessarily the result of self-suggestion.

Having said this, we must recognize that the forms
and manifestations of the Christian life in some believers

can seem to be an exercise of suggestibility that we cannot accept. Self-criticism is healthy. And this is the time to show our concern for certain forms of services, of worship, of prayer and of evangelism that come to border on suggestibility. This can occur at an individual or group level and it must cause us to review our spirituality. True prayer, as with other manifestations of the faith, lies the farthest from suggestibility because it keeps the entire personality, mind, will and emotions in a state of alert. It cannot become a routine repetition of phrases until one becomes immersed in an idea or feels a reality. This way of practising faith can border on self-suggestion.

The apostle Paul mentions a kind of meeting where an unbeliever may think that 'you are out of your mind' (1 Cor. 14:23). The problem here was certainly not the speaking in tongues itself, but the way it was done without proper order, because then it created confusion. Within the precious and great freedom of the Christian body we should try to do 'everything in a fitting and orderly way ... for God is not a God of disorder but of peace' (1 Cor. 14:33,39). The strength of our testimony is greatly related to the balance and the genuineness of our faith. If our spiritual practices border on magic rituals, in the long term our witness is weakened. People will blame our faith for being no more than self-suggestion. On the other hand, when our prayer and worship reflect the very essence of our God – order, peace, balance which co-exist with fire and zeal – the people in the world will notice that faith is much more and more costly than a mere 'life-aspirin'.

The Duration of its Results

Third, suggestibility and prayer (or faith in general) are differentiated by the duration of their effects. In addition to its evasive purpose and to its occurrence in a particular personality type, suggestion is characterized by the fleetingness of its effects. These are transitory: and the trouble that was meant to be eliminated reappears after a period of time. These limited results remind us of the action of a sedative. Once the analgesic effect has worn off, the level of pain returns to exactly what it was before. No improvement has been experienced. Suggestion fulfils a purely symptomatic function: it brings relief to a symptom.

On the other hand, the effects of faith are not transi-tory. They have a permanent nature. It is true that the first love can wane, it is true that there are crises and backslidings. But the radical and profound changes brought about by the Holy Spirit in the believer are not lost altogether, not even in times of crisis. In medical terms, we would say that faith acts as an etiological treatment: it reaches the causes, it does not relieve only the symptoms. Unlike suggestibility, faith produces changes which are deeper as time goes by (see Phil. 1:6). The successes of suggestion can be spectacular and even brilliant, but ephemeral. The successes of faith are, very often, slower, and they can lack sensationalism, but they operate radically and profoundly. They penetrate to the deepest parts of the human soul. Suggestion induced effects disappear with any influence that produces an opposing effect, that of de-suggestion. The believer is not carried about by any 'wind of doctrine' but remains 'faithful until death'. There are many differences and as Weatherhead, a specialist on this subject wrote, 'To me, real faith has little to do with suggestion.'[8]

Man as a machine: prayer, a conditioned response

This second argument is very popular today. In broad terms, it would explain religious phenomena in the following way: faith and prayer are nothing more than responses of the brain to specific stimuli. The same thing occurs with other emotions: happiness, aggressiveness and others. It is not yet known what specific area of the cerebral hemisphere or of our genes corresponds to religiosity, but this is only a matter of time. Today an increasing number of social behaviours – alcoholism, gambling, violent traits and even adultery – are justified because they are supposedly 'written in our genes'. In a recent book *The DNA Mystique: The Gene as a Cultural Icon*,[9] the authors analyse this growing fascination with what could be called the 'gene culture'. This way, our genetic code is little by little becoming 'a powerful, determinist even magic entity'. They believe that the myth of the DNA may easily become the promoter of a new – and in many cases wrong – value scale. In other words, it will greatly affect our daily life.

Following this line of thought, some thinkers claim that in the future the exact place of our religious nature will be discovered. Like in any machine, these cerebral functions are put into motion by the presence of certain stimuli, in this case of the religious type, that originate in a series of biochemical reactions. All this would explain precisely the mechanism of prayer and faith. Man is a machine and all his behaviour can be explained in a mechanical way. For this reason, this branch of psychology is called behaviourism.

This way of viewing religion reflects one of the essential premises of behaviourism which is also supported by many people: materialism. The human being is, quite simply, the most developed animal. He is the most highly evolved being in the zoological scale, having reached the crest after a long process of natural selection. Man would be something like 'a dressed monkey'.

For these thinkers the truth of things is not found through reflection but in the experimental knowledge of how and why they are produced. The psychologist, B.F. Skinner, one of the most notable representatives of behaviourism, sums up in his own words these basic points: We play from strength, and our strength is science and technology ... we need to make vast changes in human behaviour ... What we need is a technology of behaviour ... [this is] the only way to solve our problems.[10]

In the light of this school, prayer would not be anything more than the elaborated expression of a sophisticated instinct – the religious impulse – of the most developed animal. It is not related to an objective reality, God, but it all happens inside us.

How will we, as believers, respond to these assertions? An illustration will help us to clarify our answer. When a young man is in love with his girlfriend, a series of biochemical changes take place in his brain. His adrenaline increases, endorphins are released. A correct laboratory analysis would provide us with the experimental evidences of these alterations. But no one would dare say that the young man was in love because his endorphins had increased! The biochemical processes do not subtract from the reality of his love for her: they do not deny nor affirm his being in love. And much less do they tell us about the existence or about the perfection of his girlfriend. Why? The experimental description of a phenomenon neither denies nor proves anything about the truth of this phenomenon. It simply describes a mechanism, and mechanisms never explain the why, nor even the wherefore, but only the how. Making reference to a study of religion in general, a North American expert, Mortimer Oslow, affirms: 'A study of the psychology of religion indicates nothing about the validity or value of religion. It does help in the understanding of what it does and how it does it.'[11]

Even if some day the biochemical phenomena that occur in a believer's brain when praying were to be thoroughly discovered, it would not take away even a grain of truth from that prayer. We could be in agreement that praying is a conditioned response. But we cannot accept that prayer is *only* a conditioned response. We can accept that prayer has a learning ingredient and that it can be stimulated by environmental factors. But we reject the idea that it is only the result of learning and of a behaviour reinforcement. All experimental and scientific explanations regarding prayer can be exact. But this is no more than a small area of knowledge. Categories of moral and spiritual and other knowledge exist that escape the measuring instruments of any scientist. This is because the object of science is not to judge the value of a reality, but to rather discover what that reality is like. For this reason, believers ought not feel threatened by true science. It is true that the most outstanding representatives of behaviourism are well-known atheists: Watson, Skinner and others. But it is also true that some experimental scientists are active in the ranks of evangelical Christianity and are men and women having an admirable faith. On this issue, I recommend the book by Malcolm Jeeves, *Psychology and Christianity*.[12]

At this point I also want to end with a word of self-criticism. We must reject and oppose a form of prayer that acts as a response to certain clearly manipulative stimuli. These stimuli, even though good in themselves, can become an instrument of psychological pressure and with it, will give way to the criticisms that are made against us on occasion by unbelievers. Prayer needs adequate stimuli, but it can never be the result of a psychological manipulation.

The two arguments that I have considered up to here, self-suggestion and the conditioned response, have a common denominator: they are one more manifestation of the secularism of a society that has turned its back on the personal God of the Bible. In our days we are beginning to see symptoms of a new interest in the spiritual realities. Sociologists speak of postmodernism, which is characterized by a wider acceptance of new gods and other faiths apart from science, hence the popularity of syncretism and Eastern religions that I will consider in the next chapter. But for more than one hundred years we have lived in a world that looked with scepticism at any experience that did not come out of science. It rejected as irrational any expression of spiritual life. I could say that the main characteristics of the modern mentality have been rationality, objectivity, and quantification.

The rejection of the Christian faith and of prayer in our days is, in large part, due to this intellectual heritage. Although postmodernism seems to be the dominant ideology now, people are still impregnated with the positivism that is constantly exuded around us, especially in the field of the sciences. This philosophy maintains that any kind of faith, including belief in God, is a vestige of an antiquated and primitive way of thinking and is on the road to extinction. Prayer is nothing more than an evidence of this primitiveness, typical of an intellectual stage that has been little developed. When a person follows a normal maturing process, magical rites, prayer and faith, are substituted by reason. If a believer in our days affirms that prayer is of value in their life, this believer is labelled as antiquated and primitive. 'When you grow up, when you become an adult, you'll no longer need prayer.'

This is not the place to respond to these arguments. Probably, postmodernism – with its pros and cons – will be the natural historical response to so many years of rationalism. Let me just quote some paragraphs by the Argentinean writer Ernesto Sábato. They are of extraordinary interest not only because of their content but also because they come from a man trained in the field of science. Sábato, presently a writer, first earned his doctorate in physical sciences and then left the practice of science for ideological reasons. These excerpts belong to his essay, 'On the body, the soul, and the total crisis of man':

> Modern man knows the forces that govern the external world and he puts them at his service; he's the god of the earth, his weapons are gold and intelligence; his methodology is reason and calculus: his objective is the universe. The first cause doesn't interest these engineers. Technical knowledge takes the place of the metaphysical; efficiency and precision replace the metaphysical concerns ...
>
> The attempt to demonstrate the passing of the 'primitive' mentality to the 'positive' consciousness will conclude three decades later with the pathetic confession of its defeat, when the wise will finally have to recognize that such a primitive or pre-logical mentality doesn't exist, as an inferior stage of man, but that both planes coexist in any time period and culture.[13]

For modern man, drunk with his self-sufficiency, the Christian's prayer is a form of alienation, almost a symptom of an emotional illness. But, in his pride, he does not realize that there's another subtler form of alienation: the one that comes from the worship of technology and wealth, the gods of the most developed countries. The diagnosis made by God is, once again, clear and penetrating: 'You say "I am rich; I have acquired wealth and do not need a thing," but you do not realise that you are wretched, pitiful, poor' (Rev. 3:17). Modern man has their eyes too fogged over to be able to perceive their real moral situation.

They reject prayer; they reject God because, in their opinion, the only form of real existence is corporeal, material. 'Prove to me that God is here and then I'll pray.' What will we answer? At the bottom of it all, the key lies in recognizing our limitations. A human's sense organs are not equipped to perceive other forms of existence than the material ones. The evangelist Paul Little, wrote with his habitual sharpness: 'No one has ever seen a meter of love or a kilogram of justice.'[14]

In effect, another kind of immaterial reality does exist that, quite simply, we cannot perceive because we are not properly equipped to do so. The constitution of our senses stops us from doing so. Nonetheless, this doesn't exclude its existence. It was the French writer Antoine Saint-Exupery who said: 'All that is really essential is invisible to our eyes.' We cannot be so arrogant as to affirm that the only things that exist are those within the reach of our sensorial perception capacity. Ultimately, it is a problem of pride. We have to accept our limitations with humbleness, limitations that greatly surpass our capabilities. Or, to put it in positive terms, many realities exist that we cannot perceive because we are finite beings.

God is Spirit. What a simple and grandiose affirmation! He is there, as present as the very oxygen that we breathe. This was probably the idea Paul had in mind when delivering his speech to the Athenians: '[God] is not far from each one of us. For in him we live and move and have our being' (Acts 17:27–28 NIV). In prayer, God is at our side. 'It is almost a ridiculous prejudice to suppose that existence can only be corporeal.'[15] The rejection of prayer does not stem from intellectual causes: the non-believer does not reject prayer because they are more intelligent or more mature than the Christian. At its root, the problem is a moral one. Many people today consider themselves to be too wise and self-sufficient to need the crutches of faith. Our prayer is ridiculed because of their short-sightedness in the face of spiritual realities: 'Their thinking became futile and their foolish hearts were darkened' (Rom.1:22). The ultimate problem of many agnostics or atheists is that there is no place for anyone else in their hearts because, above all, they believe in themselves.

Materialism, nonetheless, ultimately leads to spiritual drought. For this reason, many people in the West today have a longing for more transcendental realities. 'People are tired of a rationalistic culture that incessantly analyses but that procures for them neither life or happiness.'[16] They thirst for meaning to their existence. For this reason, and with urgency and strong conviction, we Christians have a message to proclaim in this society. This message is simple but deep: God, invisible because he is Spirit, has made himself clearly visible in the person of Jesus Christ. God has manifested himself, has spoken in many diverse ways, but especially through his Son, the incarnate Word. The light is there. It depends on us to accept it or reject it. Prayer is the door which gives access to a personal relationship with him who has promised:

> Everyone who drinks this water will be thirsty again, but whoever drinks the water I give him will never thirst. Indeed, the water I give him will become in him a spring of water welling up to eternal life.
>
> (Jn. 4:13–14).

The Psychoanalytical argument: prayer, a childish illusion

There is a third argument that questions the validity of prayer. It stems from psychoanalysis and is based on the original concepts that Freud himself had about God and religion. Freud´s emphasis on introspection and on other aspects of the human soul are a slight deviation from the climate of all-out materialism that was being experienced in Europe at the beginning of the twentieth century. In some aspects, Freudian psychoanalysis is much like a religion and it does have a lot to do with faith. Nevertheless, Freud was not able to free himself completely from the scientific materialism of the end of the nineteenth century.

Psychoanalysis maintains that faith in God, including prayer, is a result of our need to have a relationship with an ideal father. It is nothing more than an illusion, fruit of this need. Religious beliefs are only the realization of inner desires. Let us consider a quote from Freud's work on Leonardo da Vinci:

> Psychoanalysis has made us aware of the intimate connection between the father complex and the belief in God, and has taught us that the personal God is psychologically nothing other than a magnified father: it shows us every day how young people can lose their religious belief as soon as the father's authority collapses. We recognize the root of religious need as lying in the parental complex.[17]

If Freud's hypothesis is true, let us carry it out to its ultimate consequences. Let us examine the coherence of this argument: if faith in God is actually a carry-over from childhood, an area of the personality that has not yet matured sufficiently in an adult, by logical deduction we could then observe the following phenomena:

a) No emotionally mature person would believe in God.
b) All emotionally immature people would believe in God.

c) In the measure that a person grows in psychological maturity, the person would advance from a religious stage to an atheistic stage.

d) The child, who already has a father figure, would not need to be religious because he needs no substitutes.

These would be the logical consequences of Freud's hypothesis. Nevertheless, we know that none of these affirmations is true. On the contrary, quite frequently we see that:

a) Many people who are fully mature emotionally and are psychologically stable have faith in God.

b) Many people with clear symptoms of emotional immaturity and imbalance are agnostic or atheist.

c) The psychological growth of a person is frequently accompanied by a growing faith, or at least by a greater awareness of spiritual realities.

d) Children are, in general, very open to religious things. Even when they have a loving and close father, many children show an infancy in which faith abounds.

A number of historic examples illustrate this point. Stalin and Nietzsche, among others, openly declared themselves to be atheists and nevertheless, showed symptoms of a significant psychological imbalance. On the other hand, Blaise Pascal, Johann Sebastian Bach, the great musician, or Florence Nightingale, considered the founder of modern nursing, to mention just a few names, were giants of the faith and, at the same time, were men and women of great psychological balance. These lists could be lengthened to include hundreds of examples. It is a frivolous simplification to pretend to establish a direct proportion between emotional immaturity and the need for God.

It truly is surprising that these arguments would come from a man such as Freud. His dogmatism in this area lessens, in my judgment, the intellectual stature of this notable observer of human nature. Many of Freud's diagnoses about the soul and human conduct were very accurate; especially his realism about the evilness of the human heart that is almost biblical in its vision. But, to us as Christians, his theories about God and religion are unacceptable.

As to the rest, it seems ironic to hear Freud expressing himself in terms so critical of religion because we cannot forget that his psychoanalysis is a highly mythological and deeply religious system. The majority of his basic concepts do not stem from objective experiments and clinical evidences, but, in great part, from an ideological speculation. I do not object to this channel of knowledge; it seems to be legitimate. But it does not authorize him to attack religious experiences because what Freud does in a great part of his work is religious speculation. As several of his colleagues accurately pointed out, especially Jung, 'I had observed in Freud the eruption of unconscious religious factors in some of his theories.'[18]

We accept that the theories of orthodox psychoanalysis have important things to teach us regarding the reasons why man believes in God. But this never denies or confirms the reality of God nor the validity of the faith. The fact of coming to discover unconscious reasons in our search for God or psychological defence mechanisms in our prayer lives does not invalidate the truth of its significance. Sublimation, negation, or displacement, to mention three of the most frequent unconscious defence mechanisms, are negative as long as they can distort our knowledge of the true God, and I will return to this point shortly. The fact that prayer satisfies my thirst for God or fills many of my personal needs does not reduce its objective worth in the least.

To be fair, Freud himself recognized this aspect, unlike his followers. He recognized that a belief system that satisfies our desires can be true or false and that the evidence must be sought outside, in the objective. But some of his disciples, as frequently happens, in their zealous stand for orthodoxy, came to affirm that the mere fact of demonstrating that a belief was the result of unconscious desires allowed it to be rejected as false. This argument is actually dangerous for them because it becomes a two-edged sword, as the Dutch psychologist, Rumke, says in his book, *The Psychology of Unbelief*.[19] To interpret God as a product of unconscious desires can be applied exactly the same way to the unbeliever who wants to refute religion. His unbelief can also be the result of complex psychological mechanisms.

The truth or falseness of the Christian faith is decided, ultimately, in the light of historical evidences and not upon the basis of certain unconscious and repressed psychological origins. Jesus existed two thousand years ago and rose from the dead after having been crucified. This historical information is true independently of the psychodynamics of who believes it or rejects it. The psychological life of a believer gives us data about the maturity of his faith but never about its validity. A person tormented by complexes and childhood traumas can live a faith with holes in it. The person can have a number of distortions regarding God – who he is or what he is like. But all these inner conflicts cannot validate or invalidate the person's faith. Likewise the prayer of a believer can contain neurotic aspects, an expression of emotional immaturity, but this does not discredit *all* his prayers nor prayer in general.

Let us use once again the illustration of a couple's love. When a man falls in love with a woman, he is never completely exempt from the projections of his own desires and illusions: he continues to see in her – even though partially – the ideal woman that he has in his mind and that Jung speaks of so accurately. He sees her not as she really is but as he wants her to be. Nevertheless, these projections do not invalidate that love. In the worst cases, if these projections come to be massive or intense, he is deceiving himself and in the long run will have to find out that his beloved is not as he had imagined her to be. It is an immature love, but nonetheless real. He will have to learn to see her as she is in reality. But, both the relationship with his loved one and her very existence are unquestionable.

Something similar happens with prayer and with our relationship to God. None of us, no matter how spiritually mature we may be, is free from a certain amount of idealization, of certain projections about God. A totally clean vision, free from psychological limitations, does not exist in our relationship with God. This is because no relationship in which a human being intervenes is exempt from a certain degree of projection. But that does not authorize us to conclude that prayer is an illusion. In the worst cases, like the man in the illustration, our concept of God is so subjective that it departs from the God revealed in the Bible. We make a god in our image and likeness. We do not see him just as he is, but as we want him to be. Certainly this can falsify our prayer life, but not to the point of depriving it of all value.

Therefore, the presence of 'psychological remains' in our prayers does not invalidate prayer but proves the true nature of the human being. Man is an indivisible unit. It is logical, then, that the Holy Spirit will make use of some parts of that totality in his work on the believer. He can operate as he pleases, through the consciousness or unconsciousness, using the emotional element or the pneumatic (spiritual) element. God's action upon us is integral. Our efforts ought to go toward constantly knowing better what the God of history is like, the God that has spoken and whose revelation culminates in Jesus Christ.

To the extent that God is the result of our illusions and projections, our prayer will be affected in an increasing manner with psychological problems. On the contrary, a balanced relationship through prayer with the God revealed in Jesus Christ is probably the maximum expression of emotional health in a human being.

1 *Taber's Cyclopedic Medical Dictionary* [The Random House College Dictionary: '*a*: the process of inducing thought or action without resorting to techniques or persuasion or giving rise to reflection; the offering of a stimulus in such a way as to produce an uncritical response. *b*: the thought or action induced in this way']

2 Quoted by J.M. Martínez, *Por qué aún soy Cristiano* (Tarrasa, Barcelona: CLIE, 1987), p205

3 E. Coué, *Better and Better Every Day*, quoted by J.W. Drakeford, *Psicología y Religión* (Casa Bautista de Publicaciones, 1980), p251

4 W. James, *The Varieties of Religious Experienc*, (London: The Fontana Library, 1960), pp122–3

5 Freedman and Kaplan, *Comprehensive Textbook of Psychiatry*, (Baltimore: William & Wilkins, 1980), p3359

6 A.M. Nicholi, *The Harvard Guide to Modern Psychiatry*, (Cambridge, Mass.: Harvard University Press, 1978), p287

7 H. Ey, *Tratado de Psiquiatrí* (Barcelona: Toray Masson, 1978[8]), p425

8 L. Weatherhead, *Psychology, Religion and Healing* (London: Hodder and Stoughton, 1952). See the whole of chapter three, second section, pages 128–34

9 D. Nelkin & S. Lindee, *The DNA Mystique: The Gene as a Cultural Icon* (New York: W.H. Freeman and Company)

10 B.F. Skinner, *Beyond Freedom & Dignity* (New York: Bantam/Vintage, 1972), pp1–3, 23

11 M. Oslow, 'Religion and Psychiatry', in Freedman and Kaplan (eds.), *Comprehensive Textbook of Psychiatry* (Baltimore: William & Wilkins, 1980), pp3197–8

12 M. Jeeves, *Psychology and Christianity* (Leicester: Inter-Varsity Press, 1976)

13 E. Sábato, 'Sobre el Cuerpo, el Alma y la Crisis Total del Hombre', Exclusive essay written for *Tribuna Médica*, nos. 588 and 589, December 1974

14 P. Little, *La Razón de Nuestra Fe* (Mexico: Las Américas, 1973), p12

15 C.G. Jung, *Psicología y Religión* (Barcelona: Paidos, 1981), p28

16 P. Tournier, *Medicina la Persona* (Editorial Gómez, 1965), p167

17 S. Freud, *Leonardo da Vinci* (London: Kegan Paul, 1932)

18 C.G. Jung, *Memories, dreams, reflections* (London: Fontana Books, 1972), p174

19 H.C. Rumke, *The Psychology of Unbelief* (London: Rockliff, 1952)

Chapter 5

ALL PRAYERS ALIKE?

Christian prayer and Eastern meditation

'Everything is the same: deep down, everything is alike. What is important is not how one prays, not even to whom one prays, but to pray. There is no difference between my prayer, the Nirvana, and yours made to the God of the Bible.' These are the words of a student converted to Buddhism. Along a similar line, an intellectual, supposedly a Christian believer, told me, 'We should be open to dialoguing with the East. We have many things to learn from them.'

These two examples indicate the attraction that Eastern forms of meditation have in the West. According to a report in *Time* magazine, Buddhism has gained thousands of converts in western Europe over the past several years.[1] Many people, especially in intellectual circles, are increasingly welcoming Eastern assumptions that are pantheistic and syncretistic in nature. This is yet another example of the worship of permissiveness and tolerance, untouchable idols for many of our contemporaries. Secularism also makes its way to us through this apparently scientific channel.

How are we going to face this challenge? How are we going to respond to affirmations such as those just quoted? The new mysticisms appear clothed with a 'superior' spirituality that pushes all the traditional forms of religion into a corner, including the Christian faith. As evangelical believers we need in the West today to 'be prepared to give an answer to everyone who asks you to give the reason for the hope that you have … with gentleness and respect' (1 Pet. 3:15–16). This is why I have decided to include a chapter on this topic. In an age marked by syncretism and relativism, we must defend the uniqueness of Christian prayer. A comparative study of religions shows us how, in Christianity, prayer takes on distinctive characteristics that go completely against the syncretistic motto of 'every religion is valid, every religion is good'.

One of the fundamental phenomena that take place in the act of praying is that of meditation. To be truly fruitful, prayer implies inner quietness and reflection. Without this dimension, prayer would be reduced to pure emotionalism. Remember the need for all facets of the personality to be well-balanced with each other. The advice that I overheard in a conversation a short time ago is not correct: 'Don't think, pray.' You cannot pray without thinking! Prayer implies reflective thinking. This is why I stress that meditation is an integral part of prayer.

But it is precisely in this area where we find those dangers that were referred to in chapter 3. Is any type of meditation valid? No. Meditation suitable to Christian prayer has a purpose, certain means and a framework that impress upon it a unique character. If we divest it of these characteristics, it can end up as a pure exercise of transcendental meditation or with a mysticism more closely related to New Age spirituality than to the biblical faith.

Maybe this is the reason why some Christians get frightened when they hear the word 'meditation' so that they automatically have a defensive, if not hostile attitude. This attitude of suspicion or fear, understandable because of the strong proselytism of certain cults, really has no biblical or historical foundation. Meditation is an exercise so profoundly biblical that it impregnates the pages of the Old Testament from the very beginning. 'You shall meditate on the book of the law day and night' said God to Joshua. 'Blessed is the man whose delight is in the law of the Lord: on his law he meditates day and night,' wrote the Psalmist in the very first Psalm. The practice of meditation on God's word was so essential to the people of Israel that if the title of 'inventor' of meditation could be attributed to someone, without a doubt it would be one of the great figures of the Judeo–Christian faith. In the same way, the history of the church shows an active practice of meditation, although at times excessively contaminated by non-Christian influences. We, as Christians, are the legitimate heirs of the biblical tradition, and it is therefore our duty to recover and claim the right to the true biblical meaning of meditation. This is an urgent need. And the best place to begin is prayer. When Dietrich Bonhoeffer was asked why he meditated, he replied, 'Because I am a Christian.'

Nevertheless, in recent years we have witnessed a double phenomenon that explains, at least partially, the reservations that some believers have regarding meditation. On the one hand, the progressive decline of its biblical characteristics eventually changed meditation into an arid practice devoid of any life. This brought about an attitude of indifference, especially within the evangelical Christian sector. On the other hand, cults and Eastern religions have sponsored a form of religiosity precisely centred on a certain type of meditation. This double phenomenon has caused the practice of meditation to be significantly abandoned. But meditation, understood as an inner retirement to think reflectively on God, is an integral part of prayer and, therefore, of the Christian life.

Christianity without meditation, without 'meditative prayer' as Richard Foster terms it,[2] leaves behind a dangerous emptiness in a society that is activist to the point of frenzy. People today greatly need the therapeutic balm of meditation. If we do not fill this void, others will. And they will fill it in their own way, with a universalist pantheism that promises life without anxiety for the present and utopias for the future. Part of the success of the New Age movement in our days is due to this fact. There is an emptiness in many people related to their excess of action and their deficit of reflection: too much doing and too little silence in their lives lead them to embrace any philosophy promising quietness and relaxation. Therefore those 'new spiritualities' become the Promised Land to which they pilgrimage with enthusiasm and 'faith'.

It is sad to discover that many converts to Buddhism in Europe are searching, first of all, for a transcendental life, but they reject Christianity because they associate it with materialism. We must recognize the void we have left in this area. Today, more than ever, in our technological society people have two deep needs longing to be met: they need immanence, that is close and meaningful relationships; but they also long for transcendence, that is the relationship with a superior being. It is like a deep homesickness for the original state where the Creator had a perfectly harmonious relationship with the creature.

Let us notice a remarkable fact. In the nineteenth century man 'killed' God (see Nietzsche and other atheist philosophers), but they could not kill the thirst for God.

Actually man will never be able to kill the thirst for God because it is inherent to his nature, it is impressed profoundly on his soul. This is the reason why, as Chesterton wrote, 'when man ceases to believe in God, then he believes in anything'. He needs to create new gods, regardless of their names or attributes, the important thing is to believe. Hence the great success of Eastern mysticism and the new religions at the beginning of the twenty-first century. This religious 'revival' in the West is not only the evidence that man will never be able to kill God, but as a matter of fact it is a natural result of this attempt to repress his spirituality and eradicate any sign of transcendental life.

For all these reasons, we need to proclaim vigorously the distinctive features of prayer in the area of meditation and its great value to our needy society. Knowing them will enrich the very essence of our spiritual life and will transform this life into a fertile oasis. Ignoring them will result in errors that already have antecedents in the history of the church and that, as we will see, are flourishing again in our day. Therefore, something very important is at stake.

Differences between Christian and Eastern meditation

First of all, they are different in their purpose. Eastern meditations seek to obtain a mental state of relaxation, of tranquillity, where one comes to see problems almost from a condition of indifference . A Spanish contemporary writer said that 'all the philosophy of Buddha can be equally found in a diazepam tablet!' Let us observe carefully the definition of transcendental meditation given by its founder, the Guru Maharishi:

It is an effortless, automatic mental technique consisting of turning the attention inwards toward the subtle levels of a thought until the mind transcends the experience of the subtlest states of the thought and arrives at the source of thought (pure consciousness).[3]

This definition sums up very clearly the key points of divergence with the Christian faith. The centre of this meditation is the person – 'turning the attention inwards'. To this primarily egocentric focus is added, in a logical manner, the utilitarian aspect: seek certain immediate and tangible results. Transcendental meditation is something to be 'used for'. The destination of such prayer is not, ultimately, a personal God but rather oneself. In any case, the ultimate goal is to obtain a state of liberation, of a 'supreme good', in which one's own identity is fused with the cosmic consciousness. A good example is seen in Buddhism with its state of Nirvana. This state of liberation is very much related to another key feature of our society: hedonism. Actually hedonism is a two-fold reality. It certainly seeks to attain pleasure, as much pleasure as possible. But it also has a more subtle dimension: it tries to avoid suffering as much as possible. Naturally we all want to avoid suffering. This is a human attitude which is legitimate. Otherwise we would easily fall into masochism! But the point is that our hedonistic society rejects any kind of value in suffering. In a pleasure-centred society, suffering is fruitless and absurd. Hence the great emphasis of many Eastern and new cults today on impassibility. To avoid suffering has become a first goal, almost a god. Hence also the popularity of Buddhism and its Nirvana, 'the supreme well-being where you don't feel any suffering'.

It would be healthy in such a social atmosphere to remember the words of Dostoyevsky in his book *Notes from the Underground*: 'If man wants to be really free ... he must accept pain ...' Very much in tune with the New Testament teaching, for Dostoyevsky pain and suffering have a purifying effect which is absolutely essential to grasp the true meaning of life. The capacity to face suffering without escaping it is a moral virtue which opens the doors of our inner personal transformation. See, for example, James 1:2–4 and 1 Peter 1:6–7.

We realize, therefore, the hidden egocentric motivations in many of the 'modern' religions. The centre is the person, the main concern my own well-being. It is in our interest to see how certain schools of psychology use these meditations as a relaxation technique in the treatment of psychological problems. And what is even more notorious: some of the best current essays on psychiatry present, without any further explanation, transcendental meditation and yoga as one more alternative in the treatment of anxiety.[4] As a specialist in mental health, I find this fact is quite alarming because behind a supposed technique lies hidden an ideology. There is no practice that does not have a theoretical support. Their emphasis lies in the final affirmation of the self as a transcendental experience. This experience takes a person beyond themselves, toward higher cosmic levels that aspire to join the person, in the end, with the universe. Man finds himself when he renounces his individual self and reaches a de-personalized state. A kind of a departure of the self is produced, an excursion to a different self. From there the name *transpersonalism* is given to many of these meditations.

On the other hand, the purpose of Christian meditation and prayer are almost the opposite. Their destination is a personal God and their purpose is not to reach a certain emotional state but rather an intimate relationship with the person of Jesus Christ. 'Remain in me, and

I will remain in you. No branch can bear fruit by itself ... neither can you bear fruit unless you remain in me,' Jesus said to his disciples, emphasizing this spiritual intimacy. Meditation and prayer are ways of seeking to know this God in a personal way in order to become more and more like our model, Christ (Rom. 8:29). This is the goal of meditation and of our entire Christian life. It is theocentric in that our gaze is fixed on Christ. Because we love God, we want to do what pleases him, and his desire is our progressive likeness to his Son.

Second, the means are also different. Eastern meditations come very close to being a technique. There are a series of specific exercises, a methodology that one must follow with greater or lesser exactitude in order to obtain the desired state. Christian prayer, on the other hand, is what is farthest from being a technique. This is true because of its very essence, that of an intimate relationship. 'If rules are desired to be applied, making it a method, applying it as a technique, it will no longer be alive but will be emptied of its religious substance. I do not have, therefore, a recipe to offer anyone,'[5] answered Paul Tournier when questioned regarding this topic.

Eastern meditation is fundamentally passive; one gives himself completely,. lets go. The person seeks to disconnect, to empty him or herself. As Gaius Davies, a psychiatrist, says, it 'puts the mind, as it were, in neutral gear'.[6] Here, the differences are also absolute. Christian prayer is not a technique nor is it passive. It is an active process by which the person is fully occupied with God's truth. It does not seek to empty the mind but to fill it. It does not seek to lose the attention but to concentrate it. It does not seek relaxation, but to give oneself. It does not consist of letting ideas float without a fixed direction but of setting them on concrete realities: the person of God, his works, his promises, his commandments. This establishes the framework within which meditation is developed. It is not an excursion without borders, or an aimless journey in which a map and compass are lacking.

The Christian, in his practice of meditation, has a precise map, the word of God, and a visible north, the person of Jesus Christ. Both of these reference points keep the Christian from getting lost in the darkness of introspection and of wandering by feeling his way through a diffuse religiosity. This framework plays an important function in the practice of prayer. It reminds us that prayer is not looking at ourselves first of all but at God. When the centre of prayer is the word of God it frees us from the danger of an excessive introspection.

Prayer is not communication with oneself. Certainly sometimes we talk to ourselves when praying. But this is not its purpose. Meditation is not made for us to listen or speak to ourselves in the first place. If this were true, it would become merely an exercise of self-analysis. Without a doubt, God can use the time of our meditation, as we already saw in chapter 3, to give us light and discernment: problems filed in the subconscious sometimes acquire a different perspective through prayer. This and other changes can take place because the Holy Spirit uses all valid instruments to 'lead us unto all truth'. But we do not pray to listen to ourselves nor, as the Guru Maharishi said, to turn our attention inwards. To meditate biblically, we have to use our reflective conscience, one of the unique attributes of the human being.

Let us analyse this characteristic that reaches its maximum expression when we pray. An animal is conscious; man is conscious that he is conscious. This double turn of the conscience is exclusive to human beings. It is the instrument that not only differentiates us from animals but also makes possible this unique act of meditating. It enables us to focus our attention on God. It is an active exercise that involves taking 'captive every thought to make it obedient to Christ' (2 Cor. 10:5b). In this sense, we can compare our mind to a garden. Sometimes we do not have the option of choosing the plants that grow (the thoughts), but we can choose what plants we are going to cultivate. We have to water and fertilize certain thoughts and let others dry up.

This active process, similar to that of a farmer with his fields, is what the reflective conscience performs through meditation. To 'take captive' a thought for Christ can never be something passive. It is going to involve struggle, activity. Psychologically speaking, prayer is putting our reflective conscience to the limit of its capabilities. This requires effort and tension that are absent in other forms of meditation. For this reason we will never be able to accept a syncretistic concept of prayer. All prayers are not the same.

A final difference that can be seen between Eastern religions and Christian prayer lies in the value of the person. In Eastern meditation, one's own personality is, ultimately, annulled; absorbed into a universal conscience, the identity of the self is lost. On the other hand, it is in prayer where one finds oneself fully, as indicated when mentioning its existential value. This point will be expanded on later.

So far we have considered the dangers that proceed from a concrete field: Eastern religions. But this is not the only shaky ground. From ancient times, prayer and meditation have been affected by other non-Christian currents of thought. These are much more subtle influences because they come clothed in an apparently biblical spirituality. Historically, the main danger has come from Platonic influence. This philosophy affirms that only those aspects related to the spirit are good and should be promoted. All material things are evil. From the very beginning, Platonism marked Christian mystic tradition in a very important way. One of the church fathers, Dionysius the Areopagite, affirmed that verbal prayer was only a poor substitute for 'true prayer'. 'Authentic fellowship with God is achieved in the total silence of the soul with its Creator.' In our own day we are witnessing a rebirth of Platonic influence in certain Christian circles, especially in its concept of spirituality, and here it intensely moulds the idea and practice of prayer. Those who hold these views believe that the purpose of prayer is union with God: to be so close to him in our inner being that 'I come to perceive him, to feel him as mine.' This implies an emptying of oneself, such a thorough breaking that the personality is eliminated, including its positive aspects. The believer tries to reach a point where the Creator–creature distinction no longer exists or, at least, is not noticed.

This spirituality does not reflect the whole of biblical teaching. As we have seen, the purpose of prayer is not to create a mystic state in which my self is fused with God. It is not even to get God to be present in me through certain meditation techniques. The Lord is already present with us and in us, whether we feel him or not, whether we realize it or not.

A Christian author, Watchman Nee, suggests that our spirit and the Spirit of God become so united that they can no longer be distinguished or differentiated.[7] With the respect that the work and person of Watchman Nee deserve, I cannot agree with him on this point. His affirmation is the outcome of a wholly Platonic concept of spirituality. This idea, as Macaulay affirms, 'forces a continuous exodus from oneself'.[8] The goal of prayer is not to obtain a state of impassibility where one is no longer affected by anything, not even from the external world nor from our own instincts. This would be closer to Eastern religions than to the gospel.

This spirituality of Platonic origin uses verbal prayer only as the starter motor to reach a state of ecstasy in which the heart surrenders itself totally and silently to God. What matters in this prayer is the contemplative attitude that experiences the presence of God in an intense manner, melting into one with him. When the Divine reality is perceived, words are unnecessary. In this sense, verbal prayer is a means to reach a contemplative ecstasy that is prayer par excellence. Experience is what counts. This is the best and highest way of prayer. Prayer becomes the means to feel God inside.

In our judgment, this idea of prayer being a non-verbal ecstasy phenomenon lies far away from the biblical concept. The reason for praying is not primarily to experience the reality of God, nor even to feel his presence, as has already been shown. This does not mean, however, that prayer ought to be devoid of emotion. Confession, gratitude and intercession can be full of feeling, surrounded by a heart that vibrates intensely, whether out of joy or pain. These emotions are a possible component of a genuine prayer but not a required component. In other words, what makes a prayer be more or less effective is not the quantity or the intensity of the emotions. These are not the thermometer with which to measure the quality of a prayer. Emotions can be the result of prayer, but not its goal.

Without doubt we have a lot to learn from the Christian mystic tradition, especially from its devotional life and its profound perception of the presence of God. The great mystics have given to church history a very rich spiritual heritage. But we must also be aware of errors and imbalances. Here also we can apply the advice of the apostle Paul, 'Test everything. Hold onto the good' (I Thes. 5:21).

The believer who enters the realm of Platonic ecstasy and transpersonalism runs the risk of opening themselves up to the influence of 'rulers, authorities, and the powers of this dark world' (Eph. 6:12). The English doctor and scholar on psychotherapy, Roger Hurding, writes thus, 'As well as the clear injunctions of scripture against the one who practices "divination or sorcery, interprets omens, engages in witchcraft, or casts spells, or who is a medium or spiritist or who consults the dead" (Deut. 18:10,11), we see many examples of trespassing into forbidden territory amongst the advocates of transpersonalism.'[9] These 'excursions' are dangerous because one is exposed both to divine influence and also to influence from the evil one. In observing the generalized interest that people have today in parapsychological phenomena, yoga, Eastern religions, altered states of consciousness, experiences outside of the body, etc., another psychiatrist warns, 'This urge to transcendence occasionally takes on bizarre or exaggerated forms, such as black magic, occultism, misuse of psychedelic drugs, and cultic guru worship.'[10]

At first, the Christian may feel quite attracted by the transpersonal phenomena: by their emphasis on the beyond, their constant mention of the word 'God', and their search for an authentic spirituality, which may end up blinding the novice. In this sense, the influence of certain aspects of Jung's psychology can be misleading. His dialogue with the East was, in a practical sense, a syncretism with Eastern religions, and the influence of occultism in the work of Jung is a factor to bear in mind

Therefore there is a place for contemplation and meditation in the Christian life. As believers, however, we must receive with reservation too much emphasis on the subjective. This can work to the detriment of the objective facts of our faith, above all Christ's expiation of our sins and God's plans for a new creation and a new kingdom.

This brings us to a final question: How are we to distinguish between the magical and the mystical? The former offers dangers because of its hazy borders with Eastern thought and even with the esoteric and the occult. The mystical, on the other hand, can contain healthy elements that enrich our prayer life, as long as we bear in mind the possible imbalances. One author, Theo Spoerry, helps us with a simple description, 'Magic consists in putting God at our service, instead of putting ourselves at his service.'[11] Magic, in general terms, is a form of transcendentalism that has the self as centre and goal. Christian mysticism seeks to give, to offer. Magic seeks to get, to obtain.

The Christian, through prayer, is ultimately responding to his lover, God, that is an objective you. In Eastern meditation, a diffused and generalized consciousness is pursued in which one loses his personality for the sake of a cosmic amorphous identity. In Christ, the self grows in its unique and personal character: 'You are precious and honoured in my sight ... and because I love you ... I have redeemed you ... I have called you by name: you are mine' (Is. 43:1,4 NIV). The individuality of each person acquires its highest expression in Christ who gives us a new identity, our own dignity, a deep and non-transferable sense of personhood. In Eastern meditation, exactly the opposite takes place: the personality is annulled and diluted in the cosmic swimming pool of universal consciousness.

Now, after warning of all these dangers and the evil in Eastern influences, I want to offer some practical guidance on how to practise Christian meditation bearing in mind that, because of its very nature, there is no specific technique or method. The following suggestions are very basic but they have proved to be very helpful in my own life:

- **Let the word of God speak to you**. This is the foundation of Christian meditation: 'Your word is a lamp to my feet and a light for my path' (Ps. 119:105). Once you have read the Bible text, try to understand it and let the passage speak to you.
- **Let the word of God dwell in you.** 'Let the word of Christ dwell in you richly as you teach and admonish one another with all wisdom' (Col. 3:16). Choose a sentence or a verse that you can remember and think of it during the rest of the day. I like to call this 'the thought for the day'.
- **Let the word of God mould you**. 'For the word of God is living and active. Sharper than any double-edged sword, it penetrates even to dividing your soul and spirit' (Heb. 4:12). Is there any sin I should avoid or confess? Is there any example to follow? Any promise to hold onto? How does this passage change my way of being, thinking or behaving?
- **Finally, let the God of the word encounter you**. 'One thing I ask of the Lord, this is what I seek: that I may dwell in the house of the Lord all the days of my life, to gaze upon the beauty of the Lord and to seek him in his temple' (Ps. 27:4). What do I learn about God the Father? What do I learn about the Holy Spirit? And above all, 'Fix your eyes on Jesus, the Author and Perfecter of our faith,' so that you will not grow weary and lose heart (Heb. 12:2–3).

To conclude, in Christ one fully becomes a person. In Eastern thought, the personal essence disappears altogether to be fused with the universe. Destiny seems to be quite different. Between the glorious perspective of Revelation chapter 21 and the cosmic utopia of Eastern religions, I choose the first. I will stay with the personal God who promises me with his intimate voice:

> To him who is thirsty I will give to drink without cost
>   from the spring of the water of life.
> He who overcomes will inherit all this, and
>   I will be his God and he will be my son.
>
> (Revelation 21:6b–7)

---

1 *Time Magazine*, 21 November 1988, pp54–6
2 R. Foster, *Meditative Prayer* (USA: Inter-varsity Press, 1983)
3 Guru Maharishi, *Hospital Times Magazine*, May 1970
4 As in the already quoted *Comprehensive Textbook of Psychiatry*, by Freedman and Kaplan (see page 3254) and in the *Harvard Guide to Modern Psychiatry* (page 177)
5 P. Tournier, *Técnica Psicoanalítica y Fe Religiosa* (Buenos Aires: La Aurora, 1969), p238
6 G. Davies, *Stress* (Eastbourne: Kingsway, 1988), p68
7 W. Nee, *The Release of the Spirit* (Bombay: Gospel Literature Service, 1965)
8 R. Macaulay, *Being Human* (USA: Inter-varsity Press, 1978), p46.
9 R. Hurding, *Roots and Shoots* (London: Hodder and Stoughton, 1985), p175
10 Quoted by Hurding, pp174–5
11 T. Spoerry, quoted by Paul Tournier in *Técnica Psicoanalítica y Fe Religiosa* (Buenos Aires: La Aurora, 1969), p221